Shakespeare & Biography

Shakespeare &

Series Editor:
Graham Holderness, *University of Hertfordshire*

Volume 8
Shakespeare & Biography
Edited by Katherine Scheil and Graham Holderness

Volume 7
Shakespeare & Money
Edited by Graham Holderness

Volume 6
Shakespeare & His Biographical Afterlives
Edited by Paul Franssen and Paul Edmondson

Volume 5
Shakespeare & the Ethics of War
Edited by Patrick Gray

Volume 4
Shakespeare & Creative Criticism
Edited by Rob Conkie and Scott Maisano

Volume 3
Shakespeare & the Arab World
Edited by Katherine Hennessey and Margaret Litvin

Volume 2
Shakespeare & Commemoration
Edited by Clara Calvo and Ton Hoenselaars

Volume 1
Shakespeare & Stratford
Edited by Katherine Scheil

Shakespeare & Biography

Edited by
Katherine Scheil and Graham Holderness

berghahn
NEW YORK · OXFORD
www.berghahnbooks.com

Published in 2020 by
Berghahn Books
www.berghahnbooks.com

© 2020 Berghahn Books

Originally published as a special issue of *Critical Survey*:
volume 21, number 3, unless otherwise noted.

All rights reserved. Except for the quotation of short passages
for the purposes of criticism and review, no part of this book
may be reproduced in any form or by any means, electronic or
mechanical, including photocopying, recording, or any information
storage and retrieval system now known or to be invented,
without written permission of the publisher.

Library of Congress Cataloging-in-Publication Data

Names: Scheil, Katherine West, 1966- editor. | Holderness, Graham, editor.
Title: Shakespeare & biography / edited by Katherine Scheil and Graham Holderness.
Other titles: Shakespeare and biography
Description: New York : Berghahn, 2020. | Series: Shakespeare & ; volume 8 | "Originally published as a special issue of Critical Survey:volume 21, number 3, unless otherwise noted"--Title page verso. | Includes bibliographical references and index. | Summary: "From Shakespeare's religion to his wife to his competitors in the world of early modern theatre, biographers have approached the question of the Bard's life from numerous angles. Shakespeare & Biography offers a fresh look at the biographical questions connected with the famous playwright's life, through essays and reflections written by prominent international scholars and biographers"-- Provided by publisher.
Identifiers: LCCN 2020016646 | ISBN 9781789209037 (hardback) | ISBN 9781789209044 (paperback) | ISBN 9781789209051 (ebook)
Subjects: LCSH: Shakespeare, William, 1564-1616--Biography. | Dramatists, English--Early modern, 1500-1700--Biography--History and criticism.
Classification: LCC PR2899 .S325 2020 | DDC 822.3/3--dc23
LC record available at https://lccn.loc.gov/2020016646

British Library Cataloguing in Publication Data

A catalogue record for this book is available from the British Library

ISBN 978-1-78920-903-7 hardback
ISBN 978-1-78920-904-4 paperback
ISBN 978-1-78920-905-1 ebook

Contents

Introduction   1
Shakespeare and the 'Personal Story'
Katherine Scheil and Graham Holderness

Chapter 1   7
Shakespeare and Marlowe
Re-writing the Relationship
Robert Sawyer

Chapter 2   25
The Second Best Bed and the Legacy of Anne Hathaway
Katherine Scheil

Chapter 3   38
Religion Revisited
William Shakespeare, Nicholas Owen, and the Culture of Doppelbödigkeit
Sonja Fielitz

Chapter 4   58
To Change the Picture of Shakespeare Biography
Park Honan

Chapter 5   63
   From Biographies to Bardcom
   Peter Holland

Chapter 6   68
   Shakespeare Biography and Identity Politics
   Lois Potter

Chapter 7   72
   Shakespeare and Biography
   René Weis

Chapter 8   78
   Shakeshafte
   Rowan Williams

Epilogue   123
   Some Further Account of the Life &c. of Mr. William Shakespear, with Corrections Made to the First and Second Editions, and with the Supplementation of New Matter Acquir'd from Diligent Researches in the Publick Records, and from Conversations Mr. Betterton had with the people of Stratford-upon-Avon (1715)
   Graham Holderness

Index   131

*For Park Honan (1928-2014),
who helped illuminate
the "distant and lost world" of biography*

Introduction
Shakespeare and 'the Personal Story'

Katherine Scheil and Graham Holderness

> It seems to be a kind of respect due to the memory of excellent men, especially of those whom their wit and learning have made famous, to deliver some account of themselves, as well as their works, to Posterity. For this reason, how fond do we see some people of discovering any little personal story of the great men of Antiquity, their families, the common accidents of their lives, and even their shape, make, and features have been the subject of critical enquiries. How trifling soever this Curiosity may seem to be, it is certainly very natural; and we are hardly satisfy'd with an account of any remarkable person, 'till we have heard him describ'd even to the very cloaths he wears. (Nicholas Rowe, 1709)

Thus Shakespeare biography was born. Out of the 'respect due to the memory of excellent men' arises a 'Curiosity' regarding the 'personal story'. Since the publication of Rowe's *Account* in 1709, hundreds of biographies and imaginative works have appeared, from a single year in Shakespeare's life (1599) to a novelization of Shakespeare's dog.[1]

From Rowe to Shapiro, innumerable Lives of Shakespeare have been written, by scholars and academics, by professional novelists and biographers, and by creative writers. All are in quest of the same 'personal story', but they tell it in different ways. Scholars typically approach the life on the basis of an extensive knowledge of the actual textual works and their critical literature; of Renaissance history, local and national; of the Tudor and Stuart theatre; and of Shakespeare's many afterlives, in drama, criticism, film, and the broader culture.

Notes for this section can be found on page 6.

The works precede the life, and it is the works that speak of the man. Professional biographers have a more difficult task, since the confessional material that is their stock-in-trade is virtually absent: there are no letters, diaries, or directly reported conversations; no testimonies from family, friends, and neighbours about 'the common accidents' of Shakespeare's life. Biographers depend on the same materials as scholars, but typically seek to supplement these by what scholarship would regard as unlicensed imaginative speculation. Creative writers give free reign to the imagination, and produce, out of the raw biographical facts and the mysterious connections between life and works, overtly fictional biographies that nonetheless demonstrate a surprising plausibility, and exercise a curious compulsion over the popular imagination. Here the 'personal story' tends to align with the impersonal patterns of myth and legend.

Scholar, biographer, and creative writer all seek to define the individuality of Shakespeare as author, and as child, young man, lover, husband, father, businessman, and so forth. But all are constrained by a lack of personal data. We know when and where Shakespeare was baptized, who his parents and siblings were, whom he married and when, how many children he had and when they died. We know about his success as a writer and much about his professional career. We know about his property dealings and the contents of his will. But we do not know exactly when he was born; where, when, or even if he went to school; what he was like as a child; if his family was very poor, or reasonably well off. We do not know if he worked for his father as a young man, or did something else; what happened to him in the 'lost years' 1585–1592; how he became an actor and writer; if he stayed in London to keep away from his family in Stratford. We do not know exactly when he died, or what he died from. We don't know for sure if he had to get married; if he loved his wife; if he ever lived anywhere but Stratford and London; if he had relations with other women, or men; if he was religious, and if so of what persuasion; if he loved his children; how much he cared about his writing. We know nothing for certain about the relation between his writing and his life. We do not know what he believed in; what he cared about; what he thought about anything at all.

Shakespeare scholars since Edmund Malone have tried to construct a biography based on the historical evidence, and to explore links between the man and his works. There is of course massively more information about the latter than the former, but the two are notoriously difficult to connect. While Shakespeare the public man is ubiquitously visible, Shakespeare the private man remains largely mysterious and unfathomable. 'Every attempt to write a life for Shakespeare again embroiders fact and tradition into a speculative composition that is, at least, partly fictional.'[2]

Notwithstanding, in the last few decades there has been an explosion of interest in the life of Shakespeare: according to Anne Barton's count, at least one formal biography of Shakespeare has appeared every year since 1996. Popular interest in the Bard's life, based on his massive literary achievement, but focusing on the more romantic or salacious possibilities of his personal life, also shows no sign of abating. Since Rowe collected stories about Shakespeare's youthful misdemeanours, there has been an inexhaustible public appetite for such Shakespearean legend, culminating in the hugely successful 1998 film, Tom Stoppard and Marc Norman's Oscar-winning *Shakespeare in Love*, which explains *Romeo and Juliet* as the side effect of a love affair. From this popular mythology the lay observer could be forgiven for assuming as fact that Shakespeare had to get married and hated his wife, was gay lover to the Earl of Southampton, loved a Dark Lady who was probably a prostitute, and died of syphilis. None of this colourful material has any firm basis in history, but all of it has achieved 'a hold on popular affection that no argument can weaken'.[3]

The early decades of the twenty-first century have been a particularly fruitful period for Shakespearean biographies; interest in both popular and academic biographies continues to grow;[4] and imaginative works about Shakespeare's life have flourished, in the form of novels, poems, plays, films, radio and television drama, and artworks, including Robert Nye's epistolary novel *Mrs. Shakespeare*, Grace Tiffany's novels *Will* and *My Father Had a Daughter*, Peter Whelan's play *The Herbal Bed*, Vern Thiessen's play *Shakespeare's Will*, William Boyd's film *Waste of Shame*, Tom Stoppard's *Shakespeare in Love*, and the television series *Upstart Crow* and *Slings and Arrows*.

Capitalizing on the analytical potential in this growing body of work, several of the essays in this issue were initially written for a seminar at the 2008 International Shakespeare Conference in Stratford, focusing on the various ways in which Shakespeare's life has been constructed, appropriated, and refigured in the last 300 years. Contributors consider what is at stake in the many 'texts' of Shakespeare's life in various historical periods, cultures, and contexts, and how Shakespearean biography relates to other cultural, literary, and political climates. The essays in this issue take into account aspects of Shakespeare's life and the multifarious ways his story has been configured.

Just as the life materials of Shakespeare himself have provided a seemingly endless proliferation of biographical and fictional works, so too have the lives of those connected to Shakespeare. Robert Sawyer looks at how the relationship (and "rivalry") between Shakespeare and Christopher Marlowe has been refigured over the last hundred years according to various critical and political climates, and how Marlowe has served a particular purpose in constructing versions of 'Shakespeare'. Shakespeare's wife Anne Hathaway does not escape the fictionalizing fervour; Katherine Scheil offers a paradigm for how Hathaway's life has been imagined along the lines of domesticity and sexuality, inspired by the problematic 'second best bed' phrase from Shakespeare's will. One of the key aspects of the personal story that has recently assumed new importance due to a resurgence of the 'Catholic Shakespeare' question, is religion. The topic of Shakespeare and religion is taken up by Sonja Fielitz, in her essay on the influence of Catholicism on Shakespeare.

In the second half of this volume, four biographers of Shakespeare reflect on the process of writing biography. Park Honan, Peter Holland, Lois Potter, and René Weis offer an insider's view about their own experiences as biographers, facing the challenge of creating a life for Shakespeare in the modern age.

Park Honan, the author of the well-respected biography *Shakespeare: A Life* (1998), posits several factors affecting the reception of literary biography, and the relationship between social history and life writing. The boundaries between biography and fiction seem a particularly fruitful area for analysis; as Honan points out, biography should be 'able to depict as much about life as works of fiction can'. Honan acknowledges that 'no rules govern the nature of biographical writing of course, so one makes up one's own rules'. With Shakespeare, the relationship between the literary works and the life is perhaps the central structural question for biographers to determine in crafting a life of Shakespeare. While Honan focuses mainly on the life details, he describes a 'romantic crush' on Shakespeare's plays that kept them in his mind while writing about Shakespeare's growth and development.

Peter Holland reflects on his long-standing connection with Shakespeare, from childhood trips to the theatre in Stratford-upon-Avon, to his fascination with Samuel Schoenbaum's *Shakespeare's Lives* in graduate school, culminating with his monumental entry on Shakespeare in the *Oxford Dictionary of National Biography*, the longest entry in the collection. After writing a biography of Shakespeare, what's next, he ponders. The continuing interest in Shakespeare's life, most recently in the BBC tv sitcom *Upstart Crow*, can provide solace for the biographer who has already written the life.

Lois Potter offers insight into the challenge of being a biographer in the modern era of identity politics. As both the author of *The Life of William Shakespeare: A Critical Biography* (2010) and 'the biographer who had the least in common with Shakespeare', as she puts it, Potter resists linking her own story to Shakespeare's. In the end, however, she realized that her biography told 'the story of a competent professional like me rather than the exciting rebel' that appears in other biographies.

René Weis makes a case for the importance of Stratford-upon-Avon in Shakespeare's life, depicted in the 'detailed, house-by-house' reconstruction in his rich *Shakespeare Revealed: A Biography* (2008). Explaining the challenge of writing in the shadow of other biographers, Weis contemplates the conundrum biographers face when dealing with the surviving documents. Shakespeare's will, for example, would have been imagined by biographers, but 'not the version that has survived.' The works remain tantalizingly problematic in illustrating the life, as each biographer wrestles with 'the fluid boundaries between fact and fiction.'

To complete this representative sample of the work of scholars and biographers, we have included some examples of creative, fictional biography. Graham Holderness offers a 'second edition' of Nicholas Rowe's *Account*, which incorporates later anecdotes about Shakespeare and affirms the vitality and possibilities inherent in the life and afterlife of Shakespeare, thus beginning in scholarly biography, and ending in fiction. Concluding the volume we include Rowan Williams's play *Shakeshafte*, a piece of dramatic fiction which parallels the 'Catholic Shakespeare' work represented elsewhere in this book. Williams imagines a meeting between the young teacher and poet, and the great Jesuit missionary and martyr Edmund Campion, thus endorsing our claim that scholarship, biography and imaginative fiction all belong together in the study of Shakespeare's life.

Katherine Scheil is Professor of English at the University of Minnesota. Her publications include *The Taste of the Town: Shakespearian Comedy and the Early Eighteenth-Century Theater* (Bucknell, 2003), *Shakespeare/*

Adaptation/Modern Drama (University of Toronto Press, 2011, co-edited with Randall Martin), *She Hath Been Reading: Women and Shakespeare Clubs in America* (Cornell, 2012), *Imagining Shakespeare's Wife: The Afterlife of Anne Hathaway* (Cambridge, 2018), and editor of *Shakespeare & Stratford* (Berghahn Books, 2019). She is working on a book about the history of women in Stratford-upon-Avon, as well as a book on the afterlife of the Dark Lady of Shakespeare's Sonnets.

Graham Holderness is the author or editor of some 60 books of literary criticism, theory, scholarship and theology; 'creative criticism'; and creative writing in fiction, poetry and drama. Key critical works include *The Shakespeare Myth* (MUP, 1988) *The Politics of Theatre and Drama* (Routledge, 1992); *Shakespeare: The Histories* (Bloomsbury, 2000) and *The Faith of William Shakespeare* (Lion Books, 2016). Works of creative criticism, which are half criticism and half fiction, include *Nine Lives of William Shakespeare* (Bloomsbury/Arden Shakespeare, 2011); *Tales from Shakespeare: Creative Collisions* (Cambridge, 2014) and *Re-writing Jesus: Christ in 20th Century Fiction and Film* (Bloomsbury, 2014). He has published a poetry collection *Craeft: Poems from the Anglo-Saxon* (Beeston: Shoestring Press, 2001), and four works of fiction: *The Prince of Denmark* (University of Hertfordshire Press, 2001); *Ecce Homo* (Bloomsbury, 2014); *Black and Deep Desires: William Shakespeare Vampire Hunter* (Top Hat Books, 2015); and *Meat, Murder, Malfeasance, Medicine and Martyrdom: Smithfield Stories* (Brighton: EER, 2019).

Notes

1. Nicholas Rowe, *Some Account of the Life of Mr. William Shakespear* (London, 1709), i–ii; James Shapiro, *1599: A Year in the Life of William Shakespeare* (New York: Harper Collins, 2005); Leon Rooke, *Shakespeare's Dog* (Toronto: General Publishing Company, 1981).
2. Graham Holderness, *Nine Lives of William Shakespeare* (London: Continuum, 2011), 18-19.
3. Alice Fairfax-Lucy, *Charlecote and the Lucys* (Oxford: Oxford University Press, 1958), 5.
4. Anne Barton, 'The One and Only,' *The New York Review of Books* 53.8 (11 May 2006). As Barbara Everett has remarked, 'of Shakespearean biography in particular there has been a flood over the last few decades, good, bad and indifferent.' *TLS* 17 August 2007.

Chapter 1
Shakespeare and Marlowe
Re-Writing the Relationship

Robert Sawyer

> <u>Not</u> *marching in the fields of Trasimene*
> *Where Mars did mate the warlike Carthagens,*
> <u>Nor</u> *sporting in the dalliance of love*
> *In courts of kings where state is overturned,*
> <u>Nor</u> *in the pomp of proud audacious deeds,*
> *Intends our Muse to vaunt his heavenly verse.*
> *Doctor Faustus* (B-Text, 1-6)

Like the Chorus in Marlowe's prologue to *Doctor Faustus*, let me begin by stating what this essay is not. This paper is not a detailed examination of the biographical character of either Marlowe or Shakespeare. Nor is it yet another attempt to show that Marlowe co-authored or, more conspiratorially, actually wrote some of Shakespeare's plays.[1] Nor will it focus on the working and playing conditions of the early modern theatrical scene. What it will explore is the relationship between Shakespeare and Marlowe as it has been portrayed in biographical and fictional forms.

More specifically, my essay considers the connection between Shakespeare and Marlowe, particularly as critics have portrayed them in the twentieth century. I begin with A.C. Swinburne and T.S. Eliot, then move to Irving Ribner's 1964 essay and Anthony Burgess's works, before considering the film *Shakespeare in Love* (1999). I

Notes for this section begin on page 21.

conclude my survey with Katherine Duncan-Jones's *Ungentle Shakespeare* (2001) as a marker for the end of the century's work on the two playwrights. Such an overview should show the dominance of these textual renderings and also demonstrate how the last hundred years have affected our vision as well as our version of the two writers' relationship. Commenting on the aesthetics of reception, Hans Robert Jauss suggests that such an examination will allow us to 'conceive the meaning and form' of these various works in the 'historical unfolding of [their] understanding'.[2] Ultimately, I hope to demonstrate how historical and aesthetic pressures help to shape the biographical portrayal of the relationship between the two playwrights.

The 1590s: Rival Playwrights?

Almost all accounts of the connection between Marlowe and Shakespeare accept a number of given facts. We know, for instance, that the two worked in the same circles. Both were well known in the London theatrical world in the years 1590–93; both mounted plays at the Rose, Marlowe's home base; and both broke new ground in the use of blank verse for artistic performance. We are also on safe ground to suggest that Shakespeare may have recycled some of Marlowe's themes: *The Merchant of Venice* has strong echoes of *The Jew of Malta*, while *Richard II* surely builds on Marlowe's earlier *Edward II*. Even the ambitious Macbeth may find one ancestor in the overreaching Doctor Faustus. Shakespeare and Marlowe, of course, were partly drawn to such powerful protagonists, for both had strong actors to portray their lead roles, Richard Burbage in the former's case and Edward Alleyn in the latter's.

Not only were the writers professionally related but there also seems to have been a personal relationship between them.[3] There is little doubt, for instance, that Shakespeare was alluding to Marlowe as 'Dead shepherd' in *As You Like It* when Phoebe quotes the line, 'Who ever loved, that loved not at first sight?'(3.5.83),[4] a phrase from Marlowe's *Hero and Leander* printed in 1598, one year before Shakespeare's play was probably first performed.[5] As Stanley Wells suggests, 'Marlowe's poem would have been fresh in Shakespeare's and in theatergoers' and readers' minds in 1599.[6] In the same play, Touchstone the clown claims, 'When a man's verses cannot be understood, nor a man's good wit seconded with the forward child, understanding, it strikes a man more dead than a great reckoning in a little room'(3.3.10–13), probably a reference to Marlowe's murder which occurred, perhaps in part, over the 'reckoning' of the bar tab in Deptford.[7]

Significantly, the first mention of Shakespeare in print is also intertwined with Marlowe. In Robert Greene's *Groats-worth of Wit* (1592), the reference to Shakespeare as an 'upstart crow, beautified with our feathers' is found in a letter attached to Greene's pamphlet and addressed to the other university wits, including Marlowe. While the details of the attack itself are well known, our concern is that after Greene's death, it fell to Henry Chettle, who prepared a fair copy of the pamphlet for printing, to apologize for Greene's outburst and to clarify the identities of the aggrieved parties.[8] After admitting that Greene's letter, although 'written to divers play-makers', had been taken 'offensively by one or two of them', referring to Shakespeare and Marlowe, Chettle goes on to admit that he was not 'acquainted' with either writer 'that take offense', but adds that 'with one of them [he] cares not if [he] never be'.[9] Since he eventually defends Shakespeare's character because 'divers' persons 'have reported his uprightness of dealing, which argues his honesty', it is safe to assume it was Marlowe he did not care to meet.[10] Indeed, on Marlowe's personal character, Chettle's silence seems to suggest censure if not condemnation. This distinction between honesty – soon to be seen in references to 'gentle' Will Shakespeare and transgression evidenced in charges against the 'blasphemous' Kit Marlowe – decided the dichotomy for many discussions of the two writers not only then, but more specifically, during the twentieth century.

The Early Twentieth Century: Ornate to Abstract

A.C. Swinburne's criticism in 1908 ushers in the last 100 years of critical portrayals of the rivalry between Marlowe and Shakespeare. In his late critical work, *The Age of Shakespeare* (Swinburne died the following year in 1909), the relationship is cast in the warm amber glow of Edwardian England, Swinburne's prose echoing the elegance and ornateness of language characteristic of the era.[11] Referring to Marlowe, Swinburne claims that he was, without doubt, 'the father of English tragedy and the creator of English blank verse' and the 'first English poet whose powers can be called sublime'.[12] We also hear the calm note of a critic writing during a time of English world dominance (though this was beginning to break down with the rise to power of both Germany and the United States). In his hyperbolic admiration of *Tamburlaine the Great*, Swinburne praises Marlowe's 'unfaltering and infallible command of the right note of music and the proper tone of colour'.[13] Regarding Marlowe's influence on Shakespeare, Swinburne claims that Marlowe's verses 'had in them some veins of rare enough metal to be quarried and polished by Shakespeare', the language of gems and precious stones calling to mind the stereotypical Edwardian focus on beautiful surfaces, often concealing a lack of genuine substance.[14] Positing that Shakespeare was 'indebted' to 'Marlowe as the first English master of word-music in its grander forms', Swinburne pronounces Marlowe to be the single writer who 'guided Shakespeare into the right way of work', meaning toward blank verse and away from rhyme.[15] Therefore, according to Swinburne, Marlowe is 'the greatest discoverer, the most daring and inspired pioneer, in all our poetic literature', in part because 'after Marlowe's arrival the way was prepared, the paths were made straight, for Shakespeare'.[16] Assured and grandiose, Swinburne suggests that Marlowe, and Marlowe alone, influenced Shakespeare in ways that would forever alter Elizabethan drama.

Writing during the Modernist upheaval in art and literature only a dozen years after Swinburne, T.S. Eliot presents a more complex, although less coherent, reading of the relationship, one that seems as fragmented and isolated as his own poetry. Eliot begins by dismissing Swinburne's assessment, which had claimed Marlowe as the father of English tragedy and as Shakespeare's teacher: 'In this sentence there are two misleading assumptions and two misleading conclusions', according to Eliot, countering that 'Kyd has as good a title to the first honour as Marlowe', while 'Surrey has a better title to the second'. And he adds that 'Shakespeare was not taught or guided by one of his predecessors or contemporaries alone'.[17] Of course, most scholars would agree that Shakespeare borrowed from and collaborated with a number of playwrights, but very few critics then or now would agree with Eliot's championing of Kyd or Surrey to be as mighty as Marlowe among Shakespeare's predecessors, and most would consider the statement more provocative than perceptive.

Later in the essay, Eliot adds 'that when Shakespeare borrowed from [Marlowe], which was pretty often at the beginning, Shakespeare either made something inferior or something different', but he never explains nor establishes which plays he may be referring to or why.[18] At the end of the essay, Eliot famously refers to the *Jew of Malta* as a 'farce', but he ends his discussion on the 'prodigious caricature' of Barabbas by concluding that this portrayal is 'something which Shakespeare could not do, and which he could not have understood'.[19] Once again, the lack of evidence shows Eliot reaching towards a conclusion that is never stated or demonstrated. This ambivalence and lack of a unified vision toward the two authors is characteristic of Eliot's Shakespearean and Marlovian criticism. As G.K. Hunter has recently pointed out, Eliot's critiques contain the 'power of memorable images', but they lack a 'totalizing system', instead producing an 'exemplary model' of 'ambivalence', not unlike, perhaps, the sharp images and uncertainty found in high Modernist poetry of the 1920s.[20] That Eliot also believed *Hamlet* to be an 'artistic failure' is as isolated a view as one may promote. In short, his challenge of Marlowe as Shakespeare's guide seems more personal than professional, more polemic than perceptive, and we obviously learn more about Eliot's Modernist aesthetics than we do about either Marlowe or Shakespeare or the relationship between the two.

Cold War Rhetoric and 'Mighty Opposites'

Moving ahead half a century and into a more globalized world, we witness another example of the relationship between Marlowe and Shakespeare being shaped by contextual pressures. Writing just two years after the Cuban Missile Crisis and published in the same year as Leonid Brezhnev's severe crackdown on all dissidents in Russia, Irving Ribner portrays the connection between the two artists in stark and polarized terms, echoing the Cold War rhetoric filling the newspapers and the airwaves of the time. As many historians have noted, following the Second World War, the 'only nations in a position to assume leadership were the United States and the Soviet Union', so the world 'came to witness the phenomenon of bi-polarization'.[21] For the time being, 'there was not a third power strong enough to transform the precarious American-Soviet bipolar rivalry into a multi-polar balance of power', even though Britain often tried to help bridge the gap between the two.[22] Obviously this opposition is overly simplified, for even by the mid-60s, Communist China was emerging as a significant world power. Still, the rhetoric of the time focused on the Soviet Union and the United States as *the* supreme rivals in the political arena, just as Marlowe and Shakespeare were lionized by literary critics as the supreme artistic rivals of the Elizabethan period.

But no rival existed in literary criticism at this time, for the New Critics still reigned supreme in the academy, and Ribner, a follower of G. Wilson Knight, saw literature as above and outside politics, while also championing the moral value of art. As we shall see, however, this stance is clearly ideological, for as Tobin Siebers reminds us, Cold War criticism 'introduced a model of the self-conscious critic whose greatest desire [was] to deny his or her own agency'.[23] Ribner's earlier book on Shakespeare, *Patterns in Shakespearian Tragedy* (1960), also followed the New Critical creed, explaining in its preface that the book would trace Shakespeare's 'growth in moral vision' as it developed a 'moral order'.[24]

Ribner describes the writers as diametrically opposed, not unlike the world view of many observers at the time, and also champions the more 'moral' Shakespeare at the expense of Marlowe. After admitting that 'these two titans deserve to be considered together', he disagrees that this is because Marlowe prepared the way for Shakespeare, but instead because they reflect almost opposite 'reactions to the complex[ity] of Elizabethan life, each in his own way forging a poetically valid vision of reality beyond the comprehension of the other'.[25] Further, Ribner suggests that the two 'developed in contrary directions' so that their plays seem to reflect 'to a consummate degree an opposing reaction to the Renaissance world'.[26] Part of Ribner's response seems to be affected by his own place in history, a time like that of the early modern period 'when old conceptions of universal harmony, order, and degree were breaking down'; but unlike the World Wars, with complex players and alliances, this war of words was between two mighty opposites, the United States and Russia.[27]

Ribner's literary criticism reflects this bipolar view, as he only considers Marlowe and Shakespeare – no Jonson, Middleton or Webster in sight – and in Ribner's reading, the rival playwrights look at the world through very different lenses. Although Marlowe begins with an unmatched optimism in *Tamburlaine*, with its 'triumphant glorification of human potential', he quickly proceeds into a 'point of negation in which the youthful values' of his first play are 'revealed as merely vain illusion' in his later work, *Massacre at Paris*.[28] At the same time, Shakespeare moves from the failure of kingship in the *Henry VI* plays to Richard III, who, according to Ribner, is 'capable in his final moments of a terror and even a remorse which relate him to ordinary humanity as the Guise is never related'.[29] The two writers also portray love differently. For Marlowe, love is a 'weakness' which briefly keeps the overreacher from his 'heroic destiny,' while for Shakespeare, specifically in *Romeo and Juliet*, 'the love of man and woman is an all-embracing commitment which causes youth to grow in maturity and wisdom'.[30] Even the phrases used here – 'love of man and woman', 'maturity and wisdom'– convey Ribner's ideological agenda of promoting the 'moral' Shakespeare over the 'immoral' Marlowe; this simplistic structure may also explain Ribner's refusal to complicate the reading by adding other playwrights such as those mentioned above.

Ribner also believes that any claim of Shakespeare's indebtedness to Marlowe is 'dubious ... at best', in part because there is a 'vast gulf which divides' their poetic vision, as well as their poetic diction.[31] To prove his point, he goes on to demonstrate this 'gulf' again in comparing *Doctor Faustus* and *Macbeth*. According to Ribner, both are plays in 'which an attractive and heroic figure deliberately accepts damnation'; however, in the end, Shakespeare's drama is a play of 'final affirmation and hope', while Marlowe's is one of 'negation' and 'despair'.[32] The role of evil is also dissimilar, for in Marlowe, 'evil is natural and heroic', but in Shakespeare, 'it is unnatural and doomed to extinction'.[33] In terms of versification, Ribner grudgingly admits that it is 'likely' that Marlowe taught Shakespeare some aspects of the use of blank verse, but he goes on to suggest that there is a great deal of difference between the two. For instance, Ribner posits that 'Shakespeare from the very beginning thought in terms of images, whereas Marlowe never did'.[34] And even when Ribner grants that Marlowe's plays 'are far richer than Shakespeare's in classical allusion', such references for Ribner are 'often mere ornamentation', concluding that 'the extravagant rhetorical figures of Shakespeare's earliest plays are rarely unrelated to the dramatic contexts in which they appear'.[35]

Ultimately, Ribner believes that we cannot assess the connection 'in terms of any master-disciple relationship', as both men 'forwarded' the new dramatic output of the age, each 'in his own independent way, Shakespeare with an essentially optimistic view of life', Marlowe with a restless skepticism that ended in 'frustration and despair'.[36] This clearly opposed view, granting no middle ground in the relationship, may reflect the standard view at the time of the opposed systems of capitalism, with its alleged optimism and hope, such as Shakespeare possessed in Ribner's view, and Soviet communism, with the kind of Marlovian depression and despair detected by Ribner. It also reflects Ribner's focus on moral order and optimism versus chaos and skepticism. Equally important, we should remember that when championing one writer over a contemporary, critics are also implicitly creating canons, which is 'no idle business, according to cold war critics, for it provides an ethical barometer indicating the health or sickness of our political systems'.[37] Indeed, as most scholars now agree, literary critiques have never been written in a political vacuum, nor can they be unaffected by contextual pressures.

Fact, Fiction, and Film

In the same year that Ribner's essay appeared, Anthony Burgess (best known for his dystopic novel *A Clockwork Orange*) released his fictionalized biography of Shakespeare, entitled *Nothing Like the Sun: A Story of Shakespeare's Love-Life* (1964). Burgess followed this novel with a semi-scholarly book on Shakespeare in 1970, and in the last year of his life, he published *A Dead Man in Deptford* (1994), a novelization of Marlowe's life. As Burgess dismantles the distinction not only between truth and speculation but also between literary and popular culture, we learn as much about the author and the aesthetic values of his time as we do about the rivalry itself.

Nothing Like the Sun focuses on Shakespeare's love life, presenting a Shakespearean biography full of sweat, semen, and, on occasion, stage plays. Burgess's protagonist, called WS for most of the novel, is an intelligent glove-maker's son who, early on and during a bout of drinking, is trapped into a marriage with Anne Hathaway. After leaving Anne and moving in as a private schoolmaster to the family of a Justice of the Peace in a distant borough, questions arise during his tutorials with the Justice's twin sons about the love between men in classical time. When WS responds that the 'ancients accounted that no sin', the startled boys protest that this practice is 'against religion and the teachings of Our Lord Jesus Christ'. WS replies to the boys that some say that Jesus Christ 'Himself did practise that sort of love with His beloved disciple John'.[38] Many scholarly readers of the biography would catch the allusion to Marlowe's alleged blasphemy printed in the Baines document, and the scene also prepares us for WS's encounters with Marlowe in the near future.

After WS arrives in London, he accompanies Marlowe just once to a meeting of the School of Night, where WS claims Marlowe 'raged against Christ as a charlatan saviour and mocked at the soul's existence, daring God out of his heaven'; however, WS avoided such controversy, in Burgess's version, desiring instead to 'be a gentleman, that, [and] no more'.[39] The contrast is continued when Lord Essex approaches WS at a play, and describes Shakespeare as 'mild' and more like a country 'clerk losing his hair' than 'some great roaring ruffian like this Merlin or Marlin the atheist'.[40]

After Marlowe's death, and following Southampton's commissioning of WS, the nobleman tries to console Shakespeare: 'You may exult now ... that you are without peer',[41] and suggests that WS should 'gladly lose a friend to know that', to which WS replies, 'He was not so close a friend. But there was no poet like him'.[42] While Burgess repeats the standard account of Shakespeare and Marlowe as the premier poets of the time, the novelist's flair for the imaginative, as well as his black humour and linguistic wordplay, reveal a rivalry more alive and, in some ways more compelling, than the relationship depicted in scholarly accounts. That the book also appealed to both scholars and the general reading public suggests Burgess's zesty retelling blew years of academic dust off the portrayal.

His more scholarly book, merely entitled *Shakespeare*, (published by Knopf in the United States in 1970) also drew solid reviews from academics as well as the mainstream media.[43] With over forty illustrations, some full page and many in colour, the book feels more at home on the coffee table than the library shelf, but it still reveals interesting observations about the rivalry between Shakespeare and Marlowe.

The first mention of Marlowe comes as Burgess discusses the anti-Stratfordian movement, where he considers the candidates for the real 'Shakespeare' but concludes that the 'least implausible attribution' is to Marlowe, who according to this theory 'shammed dead to escape his enemies and then, from exile, ghosted for Shakespeare'.[44] Yet Burgess concludes that while this 'sort of theory has its own fascination', ultimately it is more 'of a crossword or whodunnit order' than a plausible one.[45]

Burgess also details the professional and personal relationship between the two playwrights. Concluding that while 'Shakespeare's art did not develop out of Marlowe's' in part because they 'were temperamentally too different', Marlowe remained, in fact, 'a model for the organisation of words into swelling speeches, a master of declamation which could modulate easily from the lyrical to the pounding rhetorical' such as Burgess finds in *Titus Andronicus*.[46] As for the personal relationship, Burgess admits that while we can only 'guess' at Shakespeare's feelings for Marlowe, he suggests that Shakespeare 'admired him greatly as a poet', and he cites the allusion in *As You Like It* as proof. But, Burgess speculates, Shakespeare's '[a]ffection may have been mingled with strong disapproval of Marlowe's manner of life, for Shakespeare was a quiet man who wished to be taken for a gentleman'.[47] Ultimately, then, for Burgess, 'Shakespeare was no Kit Marlowe, drunk and ever ready to draw',[48] and to 'judge by [Shakespeare's] writing', he had 'none of Marlowe's vestigial fascination with religion'.[49]

In his last novel *A Dead Man in Deptford* (1994), Burgess returns to the subject of his college dissertation: Christopher Marlowe. If his previous two works talk much of the rivalry between the playwrights, this book nearly avoids all mention of Shakespeare, keeping Marlowe's life and his murder centre stage instead. Told through the eyes of an anonymous bit player on the London scene, this historical fiction does not even mention Shakespeare until page 178 of the 272-page novel, when we hear of one 'newly up from the country trying his hand, Shogspaw or Shagspeer or some such name',[50] a 'new player and playmaker (botcher, collaborator) from Warwickshire, a mild man but ambitious',[51] who, with Marlowe's help, begins *Henry IV*, part one.[52] However, in its portrayal of Marlowe, this novel may be Burgess's most autobiographical work on the Elizabethan period, particularly in its focus on Catholicism, espionage, and even, perhaps, Burgess's obsession with tobacco, which would lead to the lung cancer from which he eventually died.

For instance, in Burgess's world, Marlowe is clearly racked with religious questions, and Burgess also was troubled by such doubts. While admitting in one interview that his fascination with Marlowe sprang in part from 'a kind of Catholic quality',[53] he once claimed that *Doctor Faustus* 'could have been written by a practising Catholic'.[54] Suzanne Keen reminds us that the novelist had only recently 'lapsed from the Catholic faith of his upbringing' when he wrote about Marlowe in college, and during those same years, filled as they were with German bombing raids 'Marlowe's visions of hell' may have 'become particularly relevant'.[55] In the novel, Marlowe is consumed by an unnamed guilt, and in one violent outburst, he calls on 'Jesus and Mary and even St. Joseph', characters 'derived from a Catholic past', culminating in 'Oh God God God', graphically portraying, according to the narrator, that 'no agony is worse' than the 'wrenching and tearing of the inner self', a struggle between doubt and faith that also troubled the lapsed Catholic Burgess.[56]

Espionage is another essential thread in the novel, as Marlowe is deeply involved in spy work for the Queen. When Kit is summoned by Walsingham and asked to go to Rheims – a city that 'goes with Rome and Spain and hell itself as loci of diabolism' – he is told to 'listen for talk of assassination and rebellion' and to 'find out names of traitors who propose treachery'.[57] Later, when *Tamburlaine* is produced, the narrator claims 'Kit had been working on all that while feigning his divinity studies' and also 'snouting out the dissidents on Mr. Secretary's instruction'.[58] As the novel comes to a close, Marlowe is told that he has been 'privy to much that is most secret' and warned that he is 'not to be let loose to blather among playmen and others', providing the reader with one plausible motive for Marlowe's murder.[59]

Not coincidentally, Burgess himself was also accused of spying, specifically when he taught in Malaya and Brunei. During the Malayan Emergency, many London newspapers reported that Burgess was probably a part of the expatriate community that was notifying British government officials of any alleged communist sympathizers. Although part of these accusations sprang from the author being initially confused with members of the Cambridge Five,[60] one of his biographers, Roger Lewis, claims that when he himself came back from a research trip on Burgess in Malaysia in 1999, he talked to an ex-spy who detailed not only Burgess's collaborator in the CIA, but also suggested that Burgess had drawn on the CIA's experiments in mind control at Ft. Meade in Maryland for the novel *A Clockwork Orange*.[61] While this charge may be as speculative as the Baines note on Marlowe, when the CIA was asked by the same biographer when it would release its files on John Wilson, aka Anthony Burgess, he received this response: 'The CIA can neither confirm nor deny the existence or nonexistence of any CIA records'. Further, if any such material did exist, it 'would be classified for reasons of national security under sections 1.5 (c) [intelligence sources and methods] and 1.5 (d) [foreign relations] of Executive Order 12958'.[62]

Burgess's Marlowe also delights in other illicit behaviours in the novel, including meetings of the School of Night, led by Sir Walter Raleigh, whom Burgess calls Sir Stinks a Lot, and who introduces Marlowe to Tobacco (which is characterized by Burgess as 'a buggery of the lungs'), and Thomas Harriot who tries to explain to Marlowe his use of logarithms to navigate the undiscovered countries of the new world.[63] Marlowe's homosexuality is also detailed throughout the novel, including sexual encounters with the narrator, as well as the second cousin of Elizabeth's spymaster, and numerous others. Indeed, Marlowe is often heard crying out God's name after intercourse 'in some form of repentance', although, as the narrator notes, 'there was nothing to repent except the spending of seed in barren places'.[64] Religion, espionage, sexuality, and murder: all ingredients for a first rate re-telling of the Shakespeare–Marlowe rivalry.

Five years after Burgess's final novel, John Madden's film *Shakespeare in Love* (1999) also re-figures the Shakespeare–Marlowe relationship, continuing the blurring of fact and fiction as well as erasing the line between high and popular culture. In fact, one of the central criticisms of the movie revolved around such conflations. For instance, critics writing in publications as diverse as the *Chronicle of Higher Education* and *Slate* magazine attacked the screenplay of Tom Stoppard and Marc Norman for the anachronisms sprinkled throughout the movie: from the 'psychiatrist' Will visits at the beginning of the film when he has writer's block, through the spiel of the cabbie-like boatmen crossing the Thames, to the 'daily specials' offered at the local tavern. For offended critics, these types of references to popular culture amidst a film on a highbrow subject resulted in a work no more significant than the chatterings of a 'cocktail party and the emotional range of a good TV sitcom'; in other words, 'middlebrow pleasures dressed up in the trappings of high learning'.[65] Other critics, however, defended the anachronisms, claiming they 'establish[ed] a textual bridge' between the film's 'contemporary audience' and its 'mock-Elizabethan past'.[66]

I would suggest that the mixing of pop culture and highbrow entertainment is a defining tenet of postmodernism, and so is the insistence on the collaborative notions of authorship, which returns us to the alleged rivalry between Marlowe and Shakespeare. For instance, the play Shakespeare is working on in the film, and one of the movie's main conceits, is really written as much by Marlowe (and Burbage, and the Queen, and others) as it is by Shakespeare, although Marlowe provides the initial conflict and characterization. When Will runs into Marlowe in a local tavern, admitting that he has not 'written a word' of the new play, Marlowe immediately helps out, proposing that 'Romeo is ... Italian. Always in and out of love', to which Will responds, 'Yes, that's good'. Then Marlowe suggests that Romeo's love interest be the 'daughter of his enemy', and further, that Romeo's best friend should be killed in a duel by the brother of his beloved. 'His name' proclaims Marlowe, 'is Mercutio'; Will graciously replies, 'Mercutio ...

good name', and he agrees to Marlowe's ideas as he hurries out.[67] In this film, then, Shakespeare and Marlowe are transformed into congenial, and even collaborative, rivals, perhaps in part due not only to a postmodern aesthetic but also suggesting the political climate of peace and prosperity of the Clinton years in America, a period ushered in by the fall of the Berlin Wall in 1989.

Yet for all its postmodernism and wink-wink inside jokes, the film veers far away from any postmodern notions of gender identity; in fact, the characterization seems to smother any form of alternative sexuality. Yet this may merely reflect a more localized and personally political issue of the 1990s: the 'don't ask, don't tell' policy for gays in the armed services introduced by Clinton in 1993.[68] In general, and perhaps following the lead of the military, there also seems to have emerged around the same time a widespread tolerance for homosexuals in the workforce, at least for those who did not flaunt their sexuality too openly.[69]

Madden's film seems to embrace a similar ideology, for there is no mention of any transgressive sexuality by either Shakespeare or Marlowe. As Ian McAdam puts it, 'while much is made of Shakespeare's rivalry with Marlowe, there is absolutely no suggestion of a possibility that such rivalry might have included vying for the attentions of a beautiful young nobleman'.[70] Equally important, the actor playing Marlowe, Rupert Everett, is a well-known gay actor 'who has publicly expressed a desire to play gay men'.[71] Most tellingly, however, Marlowe's character, and even Everett's name, were left out of the movie's credits and screenplay, and so McAdam concludes that the sexual marginalization of Marlowe 'becomes an elision, and an apparently intentional one'.[72] Shakespeare, on the other hand, is presented as 'vigorously heterosexual', and we are made acutely aware of his various female conquests before he begins to search for his female muse in the person of Lady Viola to help get his 'penis or pen' re-inspired.[73]

In this instance, we find two contextual pressures at odds with one another. As Douglas Lanier explains, for many academic critics, 'a queer construction of Shakespeare's sexuality has become a key point of resistance to the media mainstreaming of the poet', while popular film portrayals of the Bard tend 'forcefully to (re)heterosexualize the playwright himself'.[74] Obviously *Shakespeare in Love* plays to the latter rather than the former, not only 'not asking' questions about transgressive sexuality, but, instead, avoiding such issues as if they never existed in Shakespeare's world or in our own.

Coda

But if Marlowe was usually portrayed in the twentieth century as the evil and racy rival of the gentle and honest Shakespeare, that all changed at the beginning of the twenty-first century. Just six months before the 9/11 attacks on the World Trade Center and the Pentagon, Katherine Duncan-Jones's biography of Shakespeare registered a seismic shift that altered the literary landscape in Shakespeare studies; neither the political world nor the world of Shakespeare biography would ever be quite the same in the years that followed both events.

In Duncan-Jones's reading, Shakespeare is not only a social climber, but also greedy, belligerent, self-centered, and possibly syphilitic on his death bed. In her interpretation, in fact, Marlowe nearly recedes into the background, no longer able to function as Shakespeare's evil foil, while Shakespeare is characterized as possessing many of the negative traits early biographers associated with Marlowe. Her characterization of a vehement competition between the two playwrights also suits Duncan-Jones's purposes in portraying a hateful Shakespeare, one who lived 'up to the flamboyant aggression suggested by his surname'.[75] She also posits that Shakespeare was a womanizer and an alcoholic based on Stratford gossip in the 1660s and that these vices 'played a part' in his death, concluding that Shakespeare's rise to fame caused a backlash in Stratford, and speculating that the local citizens may have viewed him as a 'mushroom gentleman' who had 'risen too far, too fast, and through a lightweight and morally dubious profession'.[76] We also hear of his mean-spirited financial dealings, his withholding of grain during the plague years, and his failure to contribute anything to local charities. As can be expected, reviews of her book ranged widely, from 'stimulating' and 'unforgettable' to 'partisan', 'idiosyncratic', and 'distorted'.[77]

Whatever the reviewers' take on the book, the publicity did nothing to stem the rise of Shakespearean biography in the years following, with many, but not all, returning to till the same soil of semi-reverent treatments of the Bard and his relationship with Marlowe. While the limits of this essay do not allow me to consider more recent biographies of the playwrights by Stephen Greenblatt (2004), Peter Ackroyd (2005), James Shapiro (2005), or Park Honan (2005), my sense is that they too will speak more loudly about their authors and their audiences than about the Shakespeare–Marlowe relationship.[78] As Jauss's theory of reception makes clear, 'every writer is dependent on the milieu, views, and ideology of his audience', and even more importantly, that a successful literary endeavour usually expresses 'what the group expects' by presenting 'the group with its own image'.[79] Therefore, in re-writing the Marlowe–Shakespeare relationship, critics from Swinburne to Duncan-Jones often offer us a portrayal reflected in the mirror of their own image and era.[80]

Robert Sawyer is Professor of English at East Tennessee State University, where he teaches Shakespeare, Victorian Literature, and Literary Criticism. Author of *Victorian Appropriations of Shakespeare* (Fairleigh Dickinson UP, 2003), he is also co-editor with Christy Desmet of *Shakespeare and Appropriation* (Routledge, 1999), and *Harold Bloom's Shakespeare* (Palgrave, 2001). His book entitled *Marlowe and Shakespeare: The Critical Rivalry* was published by Palgrave in 2017 and *Shakespeare Between the World Wars* was published by Palgrave in 2019.

Notes

1. Recently, however, *The New Oxford Shakespeare* has used data driven evidence to demonstrate Marlowe's co-authorship with Shakespeare. In 2017, for example, the editors boldly announced that Marlowe, at the very least, was a contributing author of the three parts of *Henry VI*; while this speculation was not original, printing his name beside Shakespeare's on the title page of each of the three plays was new.
2. Hans Robert Jauss, 'Literary History as a Challenge to Literary Theory', in *The Critical Tradition: Classic Texts and Contemporary Trends*, ed. David H. Richter (New York: Bedford/St. Martin's Press, 1989), 1209.
3. Stanley Wells, for example, posits that it is 'quite likely' that the two 'were friends'. *Shakespeare & Co.* (New York: Pantheon Books, 2006), 77. For the best overview of the relationship see Robert Logan, *Shakespeare's Marlowe: The Influence of Christopher Marlowe on Shakespeare's Artistry* (Aldershot, England: Ashgate, 2007), 3–8. He concludes that 'it would be less conceivable that they did not meet than that they did' (3).
4. All quotations are to the following edition: William Shakespeare, *As You Like It*, ed. Juliet Dusinberre (London: Arden, 2006).
5. See Dusinberre's introduction (especially 41) for support of the 1599 date as the first performance of *As You Like It*.
6. Wells, 76.
7. Whether the references in *AYLI* are praising or 'slyly mock[ing]' Marlowe (Dusinberre 282) remains open to speculation.
8. While Greene is still considered the most likely author of the attack and the epistle, a number of astute critics, including John Jowett, have convincingly argued that Chettle himself was the author (John Jowett. "Johannes Factotum: Henry Chettle and *Greene's Groatsworth of Wit*." *Bibliographical Society of America* 87.4 [1993]: 453-486). Duncan-Jones, offers a dissenting view, suggesting that Thomas Nashe is 'by far the stronger suspect' (44ff.).

9. Quoted in Samuel Schoenbaum, *Shakespeare's Lives* (Oxford: Clarendon Press, 1970), 51.
10. Ibid., 52.
11. It should be kept in mind that this is a sober and chastened Swinburne, who had been sent to Putney to live with Dr Theodore Watts-Dutton, a physician who helped temper many of the younger Swinburne's excesses. For a detailed reading of a much more radical Swinburne on Shakespeare in his earlier phase, see: Robert Sawyer, *Victorian Appropriations of Shakespeare: George Eliot, A.C. Swinburne, Robert Browning and Charles Dickens* (New Jersey: Fairleigh Dickinson Press, 2003). In his 1880 work, entitled *A Study of Shakespeare*, Swinburne claims that in his earlier plays, Shakespeare was 'naturally addicted to rhyme,' his 'evil angel'. But eventually his writing of blank verse 'led him into the loftier path of Marlowe' (32).
12. A.C. Swinburne, *The Age of Shakespeare* (New York: AMS Press, 1965), 1.
13. Ibid., 2.
14. Ibid., 3. The use of the metaphor of gems, polishing, and ornamentation was also employed by numerous adaptors of Shakespeare. See, for example, Katherine West Scheil, *The Taste of the Town: Shakespearian Comedy and the Early Eighteenth-Century Theatre* (Lewisburg: Bucknell University Press, 2003), particularly Chapter One (26–47).
15. Swinburne, 5, 14.
16. Ibid., 14.
17. T.S. Eliot, *The Sacred Wood* (New York: Barnes and Noble, 1928), 86.
18. Ibid., 86.
19. Ibid., 92–3.
20. Rev. G.K. Hunter, 'T.S. Eliot on Shakespeare', *Shakespeare Quarterly* 38.4 (Winter, 1987), 537–38.
21. Young Hum Kim, *Twenty Years of Crises: The Cold War Era* (Englewood Cliffs, NJ: Prentice Hall, 1968), x.
22. For a detailed analysis, see Martin J. Medhurst et al., eds., *Cold War Rhetoric: Strategy, Metaphor, and Ideology* (Lansing, Michigan: Michigan State University Press, 1997). The authors argue that rhetoric 'constituted the central substance that required serious attention if the Cold War was to remain cold and rhetoric was to be used in place of instruments of death' (xiv). Moreover, they claim that Cold War rhetoric was 'so universal' that it became a powerful 'force in dividing the world ... into two parts ... what we called the free world with the Communist world' (13).
23. Tobin Siebers, *Cold War Criticism and the Politics of Skepticism* (New York: Oxford University Press, 1993), 34.
24. Irving Ribner, *Patterns of Shakespearian Tragedy* (London: Methuen Press, 1960), 1.
25. Irving Ribner, 'Marlowe and Shakespeare', *Shakespeare Quarterly* 15.2 (1964), 41.
26. Ibid., 41.
27. Ibid., 41.
28. Ibid., 41, 43.
29. Ibid., 44.
30. Ibid., 44.
31. Ibid., 45.
32. Ibid., 49.
33. Ibid., 51.
34. Ibid., 51. Of course this 'image hunting' was part of the New Critical creed. For more on their 'systematic approach,' see Chapter 3 of my book *Shakespeare Between the World Wars: The Anglo-American Sphere* (Palgrave, 2019), pgs 108-119

35. Ibid., 51, 52.
36. Ibid., 53.
37. Siebers, *Cold War Criticism*, 32. Siebers' book provides an excellent overview of this topic, while also arguing that we are still practicing such criticism today.
38. Anthony Burgess, *Nothing Like the Sun: A Story of Shakespeare's Love-Life* (New York: Norton, 1964), 62.
39. Ibid., 85.
40. Ibid., 93.
41. Ibid, 106
42. Ibid., 106.
43. Terry Eagleton, writing in *Commonweal* called it 'Bright, racy ... knowledgeable and humorous, alternately sensible and quirky' while the *Atlantic Monthly* claimed it was '[a]nimated by affection and an understanding of the creative imagination that only a creative writer can bring to bear'. The *Daily Telegraph* added that 'Burgess's wonderfully well-stocked mind and essentially wayward spirits are just right for summoning up an apparition of the Bard' <http://www.amazon.com/gp/product/product-description/0786709723/ref=dp_proddesc_0?ie=UTF8&n=283155&s=books> Last accessed 11 August 2009.
44. Anthony Burgess, *Shakespeare* (New York: Knopf, 1970), 40.
45. Ibid., 40.
46. Ibid., 105.
47. Ibid., 116.
48. Ibid., 153.
49. Ibid., 254.
50. Anthony Burgess, *A Dead Man in Deptford* (New York: Vintage, 1993), 178.
51. Ibid., 195.
52. As James Bednarz points out in the *Cambridge Companion to Christopher Marlowe* (Cambridge: Cambridge University Press, 2004), Shakespeare and Marlowe 'engaged in a theatrical dialogue on the meaning of history' in the public theatres, while also influencing each other's interpretations, concluding that the two playwrights engaged in an 'open-ended intellectual collaboration'(99).
53. Samuel Coale, cited in Suzanne Keen, 'Book Review - *A Dead Man in Deptford*', *Commonweal* (11 Feb. 1994), <http://findarticles.com/p/articles/mi_m1252/is_n3_v121/ai_14824096/>, 1. Last accessed 11 August 2009.
54. Burgess, *Shakespeare*, 103
55. Keen, <http://findarticles.com/p/articles/mi_m1252/is_n3_v121/ai_14824096/>.
56. Burgess, *Dead Man*, 131.
57. Ibid., 29.
58. Ibid., 118.
59. Ibid., 203.
60. One of the Cambridge Five was named Guy Burgess and another Anthony Blunt. Burgess even received an apology in 1983 from the *International Herald Tribune* for referring to him as a spy.
61. Roger Lewis, *Anthony Burgess* (London: St. Martin's Press, 2002), 284–5.
62. Ibid., 401. Lewis has a separate appendix entitled 'The Cousins' where he transcribes the complete correspondence with the CIA (401–5). Burgess also wrote the preface to the James Bond novels under the Coronet imprint and he prepared a screenplay for the movie *The Spy Who Loved Me*, although it was rejected by Albert R. Broccoli in 1977.
63. Burgess, *Dead Man*, 132.

64. Ibid., 36.
65. A.O. Scott, 'Stoppard in Love: The playwright's infatuation with smart fun ... and with himself', *Slate Magazine*, (21 March 1999) <http://www.slate.com/id/22071/>. Last accessed 11 August 2009.
66. Todd Davis and Kenneth Womack, 'Reading (and Writing) the Ethics of Authorship: *Shakespeare in Love* as Postmodern Metanarrative', *Literature/Film Quarterly* (Jan. 2004), 156.
67. Marc Norman and Tom Stoppard, *Shakespeare in Love: A Screenplay* (New York: Hyperion, 1998), 30.
68. The military policy was introduced as a compromise measure in 1993 and approved later by Clinton, countering the total ban on those who were not heterosexual. According to the *Pentagon's New Policy Guidelines on Homosexuals in the Military*, 'Sexual orientation will not be a bar to service unless manifested by homosexual conduct. The military will discharge members who engage in homosexual conduct, which is defined as a homosexual act, a statement that the member is homosexual or bisexual, or a marriage or attempted marriage to someone of the same gender' (qtd. in *The New York Times* 20 July 1993, p. A14).
69. In *Romer v. Evans*, 517 U.S. 620 (1996), the Supreme Court ruled for the first time that governmental discrimination on the basis of sexual orientation is cognizable under the Equal Protection Clause. After *Romer*, the number of states banning such discrimination increased, and shortly before leaving office in 2000, President Clinton issued an executive order banning such discrimination for all civilian employment in the executive branch.
70. Ian McAdam, 'Fiction and Projection: The Construction of Early Modern Sexuality in *Elizabeth* and *Shakespeare in Love*', *Pacific Coast Philology* 35.1 (2000), 56.
71. Ibid., 56.
72. Ibid., 56.
73. Ibid., 57.
74. Douglas Lanier, 'Shakescorp "Noir"', *Shakespeare Quarterly* 53.2 (2002), 163.
75. Katherine Duncan-Jones, *Ungentle Shakespeare: Scenes from His Life* (London: Arden, 2001), 278.
76. Ibid., 259.
77. See Review by David Riggs, 'Ungentle Shakespeare: Scenes From His Life', *Shakespeare Quarterly* 53.4 (Winter 2002): 550-53; and Review by Bridget Gellert Lyons, 'Ungentle Shakespeare: Scenes From His Life', *Renaissance Quarterly* 56.2 (Summer 2003): 553–6 for representative critiques.
78. Park Honan, *Christopher Marlowe: Poet & Spy* (Oxford: Oxford University Press, 2005); Stephen Greenblatt, *Will in The World* (New York: W.W. Norton, 2004); James Shapiro, *A Year in the Life of William Shakespeare, 1599* (New York: Harper Collins, 2005); and Peter Ackroyd, *Shakespeare: the Biography* (New York: Doubleday, 2005).
79. Hans Robert Jauss, 'Literary History as a Challenge to Literary Theory', in *The Critical Tradition: Classic Texts and Contemporary Trends*, ed. David H. Richter (New York: Bedford/St. Martin's Press, 1989), 1204.
80. I want to thank my research assistant, Rebecca Catron, for her astute editing and diligent document conversion.

Chapter 2
The Second Best Bed and the Legacy of Anne Hathaway

Katherine Scheil

'I give unto my wife my second best bed with the furniture', wrote William Shakespeare in his will of March 1616, a month before his death. The repercussions of this phrase have shaped the trajectory of Anne Hathaway's life for 400 years. As an object of material domesticity as well as a reminder of sexual activity, the 'second best bed' embodies both the sexual and domestic sides of this famous wife, linking her physically to Shakespeare and to the domestic life that likely kept her in Stratford for the duration of her life.

Considerable discussion has taken place about whether the 'second best bed' was a term of endearment or an insult; I'm not concerned about the interpretive possibilities behind the phrase, but rather with how it has been attached to Anne Hathaway. To date, only one biography has been written about Hathaway (Germaine Greer's *Shakespeare's Wife*, 2007); the majority of works about her are largely imaginative in nature, relying on a handful of concrete details about Hathaway's life and a preponderance of invented moments, scenes, and encounters.[1]

In addition to the second best bed mentioned in Shakespeare's will, we can trace versions of Hathaway's afterlife to a fairly small set of other surviving facts that seem to coalesce around issues of domesticity and sexuality: the age difference of eight years between the

Notes for this section begin on page 36.

Shakespeares; the fact that she engaged in premarital sex (evident from the time between her marriage and the birth of their daughter Susanna); and her connection to the Hathaway cottage and its world of domesticity.[2] Reimaginings of Hathaway thus seem to revolve around some combination of these aspects, variously appropriated to suit ideological aims for both Shakespeare's wife and for Shakespeare himself.[3] In fact, it could be argued that versions of Anne Hathaway are always constructed in connection with Shakespeare, and that the ways she is depicted are designed to produce a particular 'Shakespeare' rather than an independent portrayal of Hathaway as an early modern woman unconstrained by her relationship to her famous husband. The terms that seem to confine representations of Hathaway (domesticity and sexuality) are the very constraints that are often suggested as hindrances to Shakespeare himself. This essay takes Shakespeare's 'second best bed' phrase as an organizing principle to sketch out the ways Anne Hathaway has been constructed in a broad sample of representative works about her afterlife, and to suggest the artificial nature of her mythologized past.[4]

The Second Best Bed, Anne Hathaway's Cottage, and Domesticity

Given the history of Anne Hathaway's Cottage, it is not surprising that Anne's afterlife is almost always entrenched in a domestic world. Perhaps because we lack any illustration of the woman herself, Anne Hathaway's Cottage has become one of the central visual images of Shakespeare's wife. Although there is no evidence that Shakespeare himself ever lived in the Hathaway's Shottery home, nor any that she ever lived there after her marriage to Shakespeare in 1582, the legacy of the Cottage nevertheless locates both the poet and his wife in pastoral, rural Warwickshire. An 1892 essay on the sale of the Cottage in Shottery captures this sentiment:

> If Stratford speaks to us of the poet's birth and education, of his years as a prosperous man of business, of the material side, which is yet so necessary a side even to the man of genius, Shottery speaks to us of the ideal side, of the time of youth's opening love, and of manhood's sweet communing with the peaceful sights and sounds of country life.[5]

Originally a farm called Hewlands, Anne Hathaway's Cottage remained in the Hathaway family until the end of the nineteenth century when it was purchased by the Shakespeare Birthplace Trust (in 1892), and has since been preserved, expanded and promoted as a picturesque emblem of rural pastoral life.

The Cottage's long history as a feminine domestic space has worked to solidify the resilient domestic context of Anne Hathaway. Mary Baker, the last family custodian of the Hathaway Cottage, died in 1899 after serving as the Cottage guide for the latter half of the nineteenth century and making tea for visitors. According to William Winter's account in 1896:

> Mrs. Mary Taylor Baker continues to reside in the Hathaway house and to show the wainscot, the great timbers, the antique bedstead, the dresser, the settle, and the fire-place with which it is believed that Shakespeare and his Anne were long and happily familiar. Mrs. Baker's pedigree, as the descendant and representative of the Hathaway family of Shakespeare's time, is set down as follows in her old family Bible.[6]

One traveller in 1885 relates that in addition to providing tours of the house and stories of the Shakespeares' mythical courtship, she also regaled the increasing number of visitors with tea: 'Mrs. Baker remarked *en passant* that though she *used* to make a cup of tea for her visitors, yet now there are so many, and she an old body, she couldn't be bothered wi' it'.[7] Mrs. Baker would probably appreciate the fact that at the extensive gift shop attached to the Cottage, visitors now can purchase their own tea and even a black and white photograph of Mrs. Baker posed in front of the property.

The Cottage itself is a material reminder of Anne's domestic life, but it also acts as a repository of material household goods from the period, further cementing Anne's afterlife as a type of historically reproduced period piece. The material goods currently displayed in the Hathaway Cottage date from the sixteenth to the nineteenth century, and do not necessarily have any connection with the poet or his wife; the Shakespeare Birthplace Trust 'Official Guide' to 'Shakespeare's Houses and Gardens' remarks that when the Trust purchased the Cottage 'it also acquired some items of furniture that had been used in the house by members of the Hathaway family and their descendants. Since then additions have been made to the room displays but the Trust's policy is to show the building much as it was at the time of its purchase. Visitors, therefore, see furniture ranging in date from the 16th to the 19th century',[8] although there is no sign of the second best bed. Like the household items that formed Mary Baker's story of the Shakespeare courtship, so too does the current space continue to form a narrative of the Shakespeares' domestic life.[9]

The grounds of the Cottage are infused with reminders of Shakespeare's plays and poems, transporting lines from the works themselves into the rural Warwickshire countryside and into a space never actually inhabited by the famous poet. The 'Willow Cabin' constructed in the gardens allows visitors to listen to a Shakespeare sonnet while sitting in the willow cabin, and the trees in the 'Tree Garden' are labelled with passages from Shakespeare's plays; an elder tree has a sign with the inscription 'Among the nettles at the elder tree' from *Titus Andronicus,* 2.3, and a cypress tree has a plaque with 'Their sweetest shade a grove of cypress trees!' from *2 Henry VI,* 3.2. Even though few items in the Cottage date from the period of the Shakespeares, nevertheless they remain a shrine to a domestic life that neither the poet nor his wife actually led in that house.

Anne Hathaway's Cottage continues to reproduce and market the feminine and domestic history of this space; for Mothering Sunday in 2009, the Cottage offered 'Mother's Magic at Anne Hathaway's', urging tourists to 'Come and visit Anne Hathaway and Mary Baker at the Cottage and listen to them talk about aspects of motherhood and housewifery in their respective times'.[10] In addition to preserving a rural domestic view of Anne Hathaway, as part of the 'Shakespeare Houses' operated by the Shakespeare Birthplace Trust, the Cottage and its associated industries also serve to continuously produce and reproduce this image, through a plethora of domestic goods available – cookies, gardening tools, tea towels, and other household items – later manifestations of Mrs. Baker's 'cup of tea' for visitors.

As well as immortalizing and producing Anne Hathaway through a consummate symbol of early modern domesticity, a thatched cottage, this image has been circulated worldwide, further embedding her as a global permanent fixture of domesticity. Visitors to rural central Wisconsin can stay at the Anne Hathaway Cottage in Green Lake; travellers to Ashland, Oregon can lodge at Anne Hathaway's B&B and Garden Suites, described as 'a home-away-from-home to everyone from early railroad workers and loggers to modern-day Shakespeare-lovers'. In Wessington, South Dakota, the Anne Hathaway Cottage is the only thatched roof building in the state, and hosts 'teas, tours, Maypole Dances, one-act plays, Christmas events, and even weddings'. Perth, Australia also has its own Anne Hathaway Cottage; in Victoria, British Columbia a full-size replica of the Hathaway Cottage even offers an 'Enhanced Cottage Tour Experience', which 'incorporates Shakespeare's literary works with the cottage tour adding live theatrical vignettes', including one where 'the kitchen becomes a stage for *The Taming of the Shrew*'.[11] Thus, for those outside the bounds of Warwickshire, a Hathaway Cottage (and the opportunity to immerse in early modern domesticity) may still be within reach.

Just as Shakespeare has forever associated his wife with the problematic 'second best bed', she too has irrevocably linked him to rural Stratford and to the domestic world he left behind for most of his playwriting career. This domestic Anne Hathaway produces a particular 'Shakespeare': she represents Shakespeare's family life, but also embodies his ties to rural Stratford, complicating the image of an urban London dramatist and poet, a counter-portrait to the 'Shakespeare' in works such as Charles Nicholl's *The Lodger Shakespeare: His Life on Silver Street* (2008).[12] Nicola J. Watson has argued that interest in the Cottage grew in the nineteenth century 'in large part out of a desire to have a sober and domestic Bard', and Douglas Lanier points out that this version of 'Shakespeare' emphasizes his 'populist origins and folk culture'. Graham Holderness contends that Anne Hathaway's Cottage represents 'pure, unimpeded images of an idealized historical past', one that is 'picturesque and untroubled'.[13] The notion of a 'Shakespeare' who partakes of a 'sweet communing with the peaceful sights and sounds of country life', has appealed to later generations for over a hundred years. Mathilde Blind's sonnet 'Anne Hathaway's Cottage' is one of numerous other works that echoes this pastoral nostalgia:

> Is this the Cottage, ivy-girt and crowned,
> And this the path down which our Shakespeare ran
> When, in the April of his love, sweet Anne
> Made all his mighty pulses throb and bound ...[14]

Several works about Anne Hathaway have deliberately complicated this serene scene of domesticity. As early as 1870, the anonymous author of 'The True Story of Mrs. Shakespeare's Life' imagines a lethal side to the bucolic Stratford scene. Here, Anne Hathaway is an 'unhappy but devoted wife' with 'an almost supernatural power of moral divination'.[15] She lives a miserable life, 'shut up in the lonely country home made hideous to her by her knowledge of the dark and guilty secret hidden within its walls' (6). Not only has she been a dutiful wife, she has also hidden Shakespeare's 'secret criminal homicide', which she discovered by accident: 'in a manner which left no kind of room for doubt, she beheld her husband interring the corpse of one of those unfortunate minor playwrights, whom he had a morbid passion for destroying, after purloining the plots of their inferior dramas'. She reports that 'it was to their lonely country house in Warwickshire, that the victims were one by one enticed by him, when he returned there from the wild orgies of his tavern life in London' (9), where he buried them under the mulberry tree. The marriage between the Shakespeares is explained by the fact that Shakespeare needed an alibi in his 'gentle, uncomplaining wife to dwell in retirement in the lonely country house' (10). In this account, Anne Hathaway's domestic life provides a cover for the ominous dark side of her competitive urban playwright husband and the deadly results of his literary aspirations and rivalries.

Audrey Peterson's mystery *Murder in Stratford: As Told by Anne Hathaway Shakespeare* (2005) also problematizes the tranquil Stratford setting by creating a plot where Shakespeare returns to Stratford and is accused of murder in his own house, only to be cleared of the crime by the ingenuity and cleverness of his faithful wife Anne. The second best bed thus becomes Shakespeare's reward to his wife for proving him innocent of the charge of murder, as she describes it: 'That brought a lump to my throat, remembering the time long ago when we were furnishing the grand rooms at New Place. He had ordered the finest bed for John and Mary [his parents], and we had often joked about ours being the "second-best". Now, out of all his hazy recollections, Will remembered that'.[16] Similarly, Tim Kelly's play *Second Best Bed* (1970) invents a scenario where Anne Hathaway is rewarded literally through the second best bed for the sacrifices she makes for her husband's career. In this brief skit, she discovers a love letter from Shakespeare after she has followed his posthumous instructions to cut open the mattress on the second best bed. Inside she finds a pouch of jewels and a letter praising her for being a supportive wife: 'If you had not been so sympathetic all these years, if you had not sent me on to London when you did, I should very likely have ended a poor farmer and a poorer husband'.[17] Kelly uses the second best bed to validate Hathaway as a stay at home mother whose sacrifices enabled the plays of Shakespeare to be written. Although the actual 'second best bed' has never materialized, it remains an enduring reminder of the domestic legacy for Anne Hathaway.

The Second Best Bed: Sexuality

As well as an object of material domesticity, the second best bed also serves as an inspiration for imagining the activities that may have occurred in that bed (or a similar one), as well as the premarital sex that resulted in daughter Susanna's conception. Thus, it is no surprise that numerous versions of Anne Hathaway have imagined various moments connected with her sex life.

She has frequently been cast as an aggressively lusty woman (perhaps because of their eight-year age difference) who attracted Shakespeare physically and demanded that he devote his energies to satisfying her instead of pursuing his career. In John Brophy's novel *Gentleman of Stratford* (1939) Anne is 'tireless in the hot response' and is interested in Shakespeare for 'the bedwork which alone mitigated and excused his idleness'. In this version, Anne was 'two people, one all female flesh, and the other all housewife', combining the domestic 'housewife' with the sexualized 'all female flesh'. Shakespeare is envious that she can multitask and balance her sexual desires with her household duties: 'she could quit the bed with the morning light and go about her tasks as if codpieces were meaningless ornaments, as if the flesh beneath her farthingale were marble cold, as if men and women had but a vegetable power of engendering'. Though Anne Hathaway can effortlessly carry out her household tasks, Shakespeare, however, cannot separate his physical desires from his artistic calling, and protests that he is 'kept like a stallion for stud', vowing to do 'something desperate' before he has 'a family to be counted by the dozen'.[18] Anne's voracious sexual appetite risks preventing her husband from ever achieving his poetic potential, and serves as a warning to readers of the dangers of female sexuality.

Similarly, Edward Fisher's novel *Shakespeare & Son* (1962) constructs a promiscuous Anne Hathaway who is a nanny in the Shakespeare household and keeps the upper hand by bedding John Shakespeare before marrying his son. In *Nothing Like the Sun* (1964), Anthony Burgess creates a typical Anne Hathaway who he describes as 'a young country woman as a sort of sexual monster' in order to produce a Shakespeare that was 'very heavily seduced and, eventually, rendered sick ... of the varied patterns of heterosexual lust'.[19] As in John Brophy's 1939 novel, here too Shakespeare must escape the overpowering sexual desires of his wife in order to pursue his career as a playwright. Some writers have invented an Anne Hathaway who uses her own promiscuous activities to get even with her philandering husband. In Amy Freed's play *The Beard of Avon* (2004), Anne Hathaway commits perhaps the ultimate act of adultery against Shakespeare by copulating with the Earl of Oxford.[20] Whether Shakespeare's wife is constructed as a 'sexual monster', a vindictive spouse who cuckolds her husband, or a crafty vixen, Anne Hathaway's sexuality is frequently a prominent aspect of her character.

Other recent versions of Anne Hathaway have used the 'second-best bed' as an inspiration for imagining some sort of connection (emotional, sexual, or both) between the Shakespeares. Carol Ann Duffy's sonnet 'Anne Hathaway' centres on an intimate relationship between the Shakespeares and the second best bed: 'The bed we loved in was a spinning world / of forests, castles, torchlight, clifftops, seas / where he would dive for pearls' while 'In the other bed, the best, our guests dozed on, / dribbling their prose'.[21]

In Robert Nye's novel *Mrs. Shakespeare: The Complete Works* (1993), the second best bed is the site of their mutual sexual pleasure, and Nye cleverly links Shakespeare's playwriting life with his domestic life through a 'bed-as-playhouse' motif:

> That bed was a private playhouse where we acted out together his dreams and his fantasies. ... O, and I was a willing accomplice in what happened in that bed, a most wanton actress. What we did was always as I liked it. Don't think otherwise for a moment. Mr Shakespeare never forced himself upon me. What we did was as I wanted it. Because now I had found out that I liked what he liked. Because now I had discovered that I wanted what he wanted. Liked it? Wanted it? I confess that I *adored* it. Reader, I doted on the act. And all our various secret plays had that one same carnal ending.[22]

Here Shakespeare's physical desires are linked to his artistic output instead of serving as an impediment to his creative side, and Hathaway's sexual desire is channelled into a creative playmaking that parallels Shakespeare's dramatic career. The second best bed has also functioned as a stage for a lonely and neglected Anne Hathaway, highlighting the fact that she survived as a single mother for nearly two decades without her husband in permanent residence. In her poem 'Anne Hathaway', Elizabeth Jones imagines a self-satisfying Anne Hathaway, who 'compensating for his absence, / masturbates in iambic pentameter / on the second best bed'.[23]

One of the most extended treatments of the domesticity and sexuality associated with Anne Hathaway occurs in Renaissance scholar and novelist Grace Tiffany's two works *My Father Had a Daughter*:

Judith Shakespeare's Tale (2003) and *Will: A Novel* (2004). In both novels, Anne Hathaway is a strong-minded maternal figure who disparages her husband's playwriting career, complaining to her daughter Judith that Shakespeare 'was in London hunched over a table in an ill-lit room jotting away, a thing he could just as well do at home but had chosen not to'.[24]

Anne Hathaway is introduced in the novel *Will* in a scene immediately linking her to the familiar tropes of domesticity and sexuality. When we first meet Anne Hathaway, she is about to be cast out from her comfortable domestic life: 'In the dark days after the cow fell on old Richard Hathaway, daughter Anne had been let to know by her brother, the farm's inheritor, that he'd no will to house her much longer' (19). She then meets Shakespeare, who kisses her, though 'he was not the first to do that, or to do what he did soon after' (23). She 'found it hard to say him nay', and within a year 'the loud-lunged babe lay yelling in Anne's arms or in this spot or that of the cramped Henley Street home while its mother bustled about her new duties' (23). Within the first dozen pages of the novel, Anne is ensconced once again in a domestic scene trapped by the product of her sexual promiscuity.

Will contains perhaps the most extensive use of the bed motif throughout the novel, as a touchstone for the tensions between domesticity and sexuality in the Shakespeare marriage. Shortly after their marriage, the Shakespeares 'slept in his parents' old wedding bed with its carved headboard, under the image of Adam and Eve and the fork-tongued snake' (23), its overt symbolism foreshadowing the eventual fall and later redemption of the playwright through his wife at the end of the work.

Throughout the novel, the Shakespeares return to the Paradise bed, and it functions as a domestic space to articulate their changing relationship and as a reminder of the physical bond between them and its eventual deterioration. When Will returns to Stratford on one of his trips from London, he 'lay with Anne in the Paradise bed. With one hand he clasped his wife's, and with the other he traced, above and behind him, the carved image of the Tree of Knowledge. He felt the body of the serpent, coiled around the trunk, half-hidden under the wooden leaves' (78). As Will's playwriting career takes off, it becomes even more difficult for him to reconcile his domestic life in Stratford with his wife. On one trip home, Anne joined Will in bed and 'found him staring at the thatched ceiling with one arm resting against the oaken headboard of their bed. His fingers traced the serpent's shape on the carved scene of Paradise' (118). This scene presages their eventual separation, articulated through separate beds. Alone in Stratford, 'Anne lay in the Paradise bed below the carving of the snake. Her body stiffened whenever she thought of her husband, which was more often than she liked'. Likewise, Shakespeare sleeps alone in a bed in London, bereft of the domestic comforts of the Stratford bed: he 'lay on a straw mattress in Silver Street, suffering its scratchy ticking. He thought of Anne and of many other things too, as he dreamed a new play. The space between London and Stratford did not melt, and their two-ness was not transcended' (366).

When they next meet in Stratford, their separation is staged in the bed: 'That night Will lay in the Paradise bed while Anne slept huddled far on its western edge. He stared at the ceiling and dreamed a waking dream ... He opened his lids, frightened by himself and his fancy. Anne breathed in the bed beside him. He reached to touch her shoulder, but before he reached her he pulled his hand back, and touched the carved headboard instead' (397). When the Globe burns at the end of the novel, Anne saves Shakespeare from the fire and forgives him for his infidelities; 'In her arms he became human, and wept' (403). The novel ends before Shakespeare's death, but presumably their last-minute reconciliation suggests that the Paradise bed will be bequeathed to Anne in the will. In this extended treatment, the bed takes on a larger significance, as the barometer of intimacy, betrayal, and perseverance in the Shakespeare marriage. In Tiffany's work, the bed is a complex arena where the domestic and sexual sides of Shakespeare and his wife intertwine, conflict, and eventually resolve.

Conclusion: 'The broad silver gilt bowl' and Other Possibilities

We have seen how versions of Anne Hathaway's afterlife have relied on her inheritance of the second best bed, her status as an older woman, her engagement in premarital sex, and her association with the domestic space of the Hathaway family home. There are, of course, other factors that have shaped her afterlife, but these seem to be the most prevalent and influential. One additional component of her legacy, and perhaps the most obvious, is her identity as Shakespeare's wife. It might be worth pondering the degree to which she is of interest because of her position as wife of the most famous playwright and author. Can Anne Hathaway ever be anything more than a fabricated 'Shakespeare's wife'? Is her attachment to Shakespeare through their marriage inescapable — is she always viewed in connection to him, or can she ever escape from the role of 'Shakespeare's wife'? Even Germaine Greer's recent biography is titled *Shakespeare's Wife*, rather than 'Anne Hathaway: A Biography'. In fact, when Greer attempts to move beyond the confines of the parameters outlined in this essay to suggest that Hathaway may have been a financially independent woman involved in a number of investments (including the First Folio), she even refers to such a suggestion as 'absurd' (146), a mild description compared to the reactions of some reviewers of the book.[25]

It might also be worth contemplating what the afterlife of Anne Hathaway might have been like, had she been allocated something different in her husband's will. What if, for example, she was given the 'broad silver gilt bowl' that daughter Judith receives in the same line of the will, instead of the 'second best bed'. Similarly, we might ask how 'Anne Hathaway' might have been constructed differently if the Hathaway family home had not survived, or had been purchased by a private individual instead of by the Shakespeare Birthplace Trust in 1892?

Likewise, if Francis Gastrell hadn't destroyed New Place in 1759 out of frustration with the growing Stratford tourist trade, how would that have conditioned the way material spaces (particularly of tourism) determine afterlives? If tourists flocked to New Place, Shakespeare's retirement home on Chapel Street in Stratford instead of making the pilgrimage walk to Shottery and the thatched cottage filled with domestic items and English gardens, how might the legacy of 'Anne Hathaway' have been different? These questions are impossible to answer, but they do offer a useful exercise in underlining how the material circumstances of history (like beds and wills) affect the later reconstruction of lives.

Katherine Scheil is Professor of English at the University of Minnesota. Her publications include *The Taste of the Town: Shakespearian Comedy and the Early Eighteenth-Century Theater* (Bucknell, 2003), *Shakespeare/Adaptation/Modern Drama* (University of Toronto Press, 2011, co-edited with Randall Martin), *She Hath Been Reading: Women and Shakespeare Clubs in America* (Cornell, 2012), *Imagining Shakespeare's Wife: The Afterlife of Anne Hathaway* (Cambridge, 2018), and editor of *Shakespeare & Stratford* (Berghahn Books, 2019). She is working on a book about the history of women in Stratford-upon-Avon, as well as a book on the afterlife of the Dark Lady of Shakespeare's Sonnets.

Notes

1. I offer a lengthier exploration of the imaginative afterlife of Anne Hathaway in *Imagining Shakespeare's Wife: The Afterlife of Anne Hathaway* (Cambridge, 2018). This essay was an early version of what later became a book-length study.
2. In the article '"We Begin to be interested in Mrs. S": Male Representations of Anne Hathaway in Fictional Biographies of Shakespeare', Enno Ruge argues that 'in a growing number of apologetic narratives mostly written by men Anne Hathaway features as the sexually experienced woman who seduced the innocent boy of eighteen to trick him into marriage only to turn out a begging, possibly unfaithful wife with a tendency towards Puritanism' (412). Ruge focuses only on three fictional portraits of Anne Hathaway: the 'latent misogyny' in Joyce's 'Scylla and Charybdis' chapter in *Ulysses* (1922), Burgess's *Nothing Like the Sun* (1964), and the 'counter-narrative' of Robert Nye's *Mrs. Shakespeare* (1993). *Zeitschrift für Anglistik und Amerikanistik* 50 (2002), 411–22.
3. Graham Holderness points out that the 'cultural reconstruction' of Shakespeare's life involves a long history of appropriation 'in the service of various ideologies and political interests'. *Cultural Shakespeare: Essays in the Shakespeare Myth* (Hertfordshire: University of Hertfordshire Press, 2001), 4. The same could be said about Shakespeare's wife.
4. I have discussed the domestic world of Anne Hathaway in recent stage versions and biographies, in 'Filling in the "Wife-Shaped Void": The Contemporary Afterlife of Anne Hathaway', in *Shakespeare Survey* 63 (2010), 225-236. See also Barbara Hodgdon, *The Shakespeare Trade* (Philadelphia: University of Pennsylvania Press, 1998) and Marjorie Garbe, *Profiling Shakespeare* (New York: Routledge, 2008).
5. 'Anne Hathaway's Cottage'. *All the Year Round* (30 April 1892), 420. Nicola J. Watson provides an excellent discussion of Anne Hathaway's Cottage in 'Shakespeare on the Tourist Trail', in *The Cambridge Companion to Shakespeare and Popular Culture*, ed. Robert Shaughnessy (Cambridge: Cambridge University Press, 2007), 199–226.
6. William Winter, *Old Shrines and Ivy* (New York and London: Macmillan, 1896), 43–4.
7. E. Poingdestre, 'A Summer Day at Stratford-on-Avon'. *Temple Bar Magazine* (May 1885). Reprinted in *Littell's Living Age*, fifth series, volume 50 (April–June 1885), 635.
8. *The Shakespeare Houses* (Norwich: Jarrold Publishing, 2008), 21.
9. On a visit in August 2008, my tour guide repeatedly used the phrase "we like to believe" when narrating the story of the Shakespeares' courtship at the Hathaway Cottage.
10. <http://www.visitstratforduponavon.co.uk/eventdetails.php?eventid=68>. Last accessed 11 August 2009.

11. See <http://www.annehathawaycottage.com/home.shtml>; <http://www.shakespearegarden.org/>; <http://www.victorialodging.com/attraction/anne-hathaways-cottage>. Last accessed 11 August 2009.
12. Charles Nicholl, *The Lodger Shakespeare: His Life on Silver Street* (New York: Viking, 2008).
13. Nicola J. Watson, 'Shakespeare on the Tourist Trail', 211; Douglas Lanier, 'Shakespeare™: Myth and Biographical Fiction', in *The Cambridge Companion to Shakespeare and Popular Culture*, 101; Graham Holderness, *Cultural Shakespeare*, 131.
14. *The Poetical Works of Mathilde Blind*, ed. Arthur Symons (London: T. Fisher Unwin, 1900), 439.
15. *The True Story of Mrs. Shakespeare's Life* (Boston: Loring, 1870), 5. The essay originally appeared in *The Gentleman's Magazine* of December 1869 as a satire on Harriet Beecher Stowe's 'The True Story of Lady Byron's Life'.
16. Audrey Peterson, *Murder in Stratford: As Told by Anne Hathaway Shakespeare* (Waterville, Maine: Five Star, 2005), 211.
17. Tim Kelly, *Second Best Bed: A Romantic Speculation in One Act for Eight Girls* (New York: Dramatists Play Service, 1970), 15.
18. John Brophy, *Gentleman of Stratford: A Novel* (New York: Harper, 1940), 66–7.
19. Edward Fisher, *Shakespeare & Son* (New York: Abelard-Schuman, 1962); Anthony Burgess, 'Genesis and Headache', in *Afterwords*, ed. Thomas McCormack (New York: Harper and Row, 1969), 36.
20. I offer a lengthier discussion of this play in "Filling in the 'Wife-Shaped Void": The Contemporary Afterlife of Anne Hathaway', *Shakespeare Survey* 63.
21. Carol Ann Duffy, 'Anne Hathaway', in *The World's Wife* (London: Faber & Faber, 2000).
22. Robert Nye, *Mrs. Shakespeare: The Complete Works* (Sevenoaks: Sceptre, 1993), 181–2.
23. Elizabeth Jones, 'Anne Hathaway'. *The Claremont Review* 16 (1999), 17–18.
24. Grace Tiffany, *My Father Had a Daughter: Judith Shakespeare's Tale* (New York: Penguin, 2003), 19–20; *Will: A Novel* (New York: Berkley Books, 2004).
25. For example, Peter Conrad calls Greer's biography a 'reckless, baseless' product of her 'wild-eyed, foamy-lipped enthusiasm' in 'Dr. Greer on the Warpath', *The Observer*, 2 September 2007.

Chapter 3
Religion Revisited
William Shakespeare, Nicholas Owen,
and the Culture of *Doppelbödigkeit*

Sonja Fielitz

This article[1] engages with the so-called 'visual turn' in the humanities and reflects on early modern religious matters, that is, William Shakespeare, and the Jesuits' use of things visual in the fields of arts[2] as well as architecture.[3] In the following, I will synthesize two seemingly disparate fields, respectively personalities, i.e., the British Bard (addressing the question of his religious orientation as well as his literary work), and Nicholas Owen, the master-builder of Jesuit priest-holes of the time. As I will propose, the *tertium comparationis* could be the culture of *Doppelbödigkeit*.[4] According to my knowledge, this topic has not been pursued to date. What I will not do in this article in the context of Shakespeare's biography, however, is to trace further possible Catholic influences on him,[5] nor maintain that he was a Catholic.

Introduction: Early Modern Religious Discourses

Criticism

Religion appears to have been one of the most crucial topics in the early modern period:

> On 19 December 1601, John Croke, then Speaker of the House of Commons, addressed his colleagues: 'If a question should be asked,

Notes for this section begin on page 52.

> What is the first and chief thing in a Commonwealth to be regarded?
> I should say, religion. If, What is the second, I should say, religion. If,
> What the third? I should say, religion.[6]

In John Florio's 1603 translation, Montaigne had called religion 'the most important subject, that possibly can be' and noted that in England the official forms or worship had 'been changed and re-changed three or foure times,' Certainly early modern England saw its official religion ... in whatever shapes it was experienced, ... as prominent and persistent.'[7]

Since the 1990s, the topic of *Shakespeare and Religion* has seen a vibrant revival in literary criticism, and the most popular title may have been Stephen Greenblatt's *Will in the World* of 2004. Furthermore (to name but a few), the studies by Christopher Baker, Jonathan Dollimore and Terry Eagleton, Stephen Greenblatt, Gary Taylor, Alexandra Walsham[8], and more recently June Schlueter and Dennis McCarthy[9] have enriched our knowledge of early modern religious discourses and the British Bard.

Numerous studies have also been written on one special aspect of the early modern Catholic discourse, that is, the Jesuit mission. Since Richard Wilson's *TLS* article of 19 December 1997, the topic which had earlier been discussed by Richard Simpson (*The Rambler* 1854 and *Edinburgh Review* 1866), Christopher Baker (1937), E.K. Chambers (1944), and Ernest Honigmann,[10] as well as Peter Milward and Anthony Holden[11] in the 1970s to 1990s has been brought back to public and critical discussion. If, as Wilson claims, the William Shakeshafte of Alexander Houghton's will of 3 August 1581 is identical with William Shakespeare,[12] the dramatist would have been in close contact with one of the most central and influential Catholic families of the time. Whether this be the case or not, Wilson's essay certainly sparked fresh interest in the question of Shakespeare's religious orientation. Further publications in this field include titles by Ernst Honigmann, Gerard Kilroy, Arthur Marotti, Thomas McCoog S.J., Alison Shell, Paul Whitfield White,[13] Richard Dutton, Alison Findlay and Richard Wilson,[14] and, most recently, Thomas Alfred, Lowell Gallagher, Peter Iver Kaufmann, James E. Kelly and Susan Royal[15], and the indefatigable Thomas McCoog SJ.[16] They include analyses, editions of manuscripts and printed sources[17] as well as collections of essays such as the one edited by Graham Holderness and Katherine Scheil.[18]

Shakespeare and the Old Faith

The assumption that the traditions of the Old Faith were rather strong around Stratford-upon-Avon, where William Shakespeare was raised, is not a recent one.[19] This region has long been known as a stronghold of recusancy and Catholic resistance. Within Shakespeare's personal family context, his mother's side was Catholic, and that he no longer attended Anglican services from the late 1570s onwards, may be due to his possible conversion by the first Jesuit missionary priests who had penetrated to the vicinity of Stratford-upon-Avon by 1580. Furthermore, in 1606, William Shakespeare's elder daughter Susanna was accused for refusing to take communion.[20] 'How strong recusancy was in Worcestershire is shown by the examination of John Felton, an old Marian priest who was brought before Bishop Whitgift at Worcester on Christmas Eve 1582. He listed by name thirteen places in Worcestershire where he had ministered during the previous ten years, together with one in Hertfordshire and one in Gloucestershire.'[21] What is more, a substantial number of conspirators of the Gunpowder Plot came from the area. 'Sir Edward Bushell, a cousin of the Wintours of Huddington, was seen just before the Gunpowder Plot with Robert Catesby at Clopton House, near Stratford, which Ambrose Rockwood [of Coldham in Suffolk] had rented at Michaelmas 1605 [in order to be on the spot]' (Hodgetts, *Secret Hiding Places* 78, 162). Furthermore, a certificate of Warwickshire recusants dated 25 September 1592 tells us that

> Thomas Bates, whome we certified to our Lordshipps in our first certificatt to have brought a man Childe to the house of Mrs Edwards in Tanworth in this Country, Dwelled then in Lapworthe and was there presented for a Recusant, and is on the 20th of September 1592 presented for a Willfull Recusante by the presenters of Stratford uppon Avon dwelling at Lapworth Hall alias Bushwood Hall within theare parrishe.[22]

Thomas Bates was the Gunpowder conspirator and the servant of Robert Catesby, who was born at Bushwood Hall, three miles west of Baddesley. Tanworth-in-Arden is five miles west of Baddesley Clinton, and Baddesley Clinton itself is ninety-nine miles from London and eighteen (a day's ride) from Hindlip. Bushwood Hall is ten miles away from Stratford (Hodgetts, 'Elizabethan Pries-Holes III', 182f.).

Another important critical issue in this field, which, however – for reasons of space – cannot be included in this essay, is John Shakespeare's[23] so-called Spiritual Testament, an overtly Catholic declaration of faith linked to the early English Jesuit mission in 1580/81, which was discovered hidden in the rafters of his house in the Birthplace in Stratford-upon-Avon in 1757.[24] Furthermore, interpretations of individual dramas against a religious background, which have significantly increased over the last few decades, must be omitted here as well.[25]

The Visual Language of the Order of the Jesuits

The Society of Jesus[26], founded in 1540 by the Spaniard Ignatius of Loyola (c. 1491-1556), has long used works of art and architecture, as well as other aspects of visual and material culture[27] for varied purposes[28], because the Society quickly recognized and utilized the visual arts as a powerful tool of communication.[29] 'The Jesuit investment in images, whether verbal or visual, virtual or actual, pictorial or poetic, rhetorical or exegetical, was strong and sustained, and may perhaps even be identified as one of the order's defining characteristics.'[30] Ignatius believed that a visualization of the scene would engage all of the senses[31] and facilitate a better understanding of the life and teachings of Christ. As we will see in more detail below,

> the commissioning of a vast number of illustrated printed works, the extensive building and decoration of churches (and other structures including professed houses, schools, and colleges) all over the world, and the production of marvellous theatrical spectacles, speaks to the Society's desire to engage the world with a visual language, in addition to spoken and written ones.[32]

Nicholas Owen (c 1555-1606)

The Society of Jesus' visual artists responsible for producing more permanent and external works 'engaged the spectator ... in vivid color, with daring illusionism, of innovative compositions, or possessing unexpected symbolism'.[33] Perhaps the most gifted one of these artists in the field of architecture, was Nicholas Owen, who might not be familiar to many (early modern) scholars and critics.[34] He was a Jesuit brother and *the* master-builder of priest holes, that is, concealed hiding places in the homes of Catholics designed to hide priests from the authorities.[35] He thus enabled Jesuits and other fugitives from being captured by the Sovereign's priest hunters. Andreas Eucaemon-Ioannes called him 'latibulorum egregious artifex' ['excellent master of hiding holes'; *my translation*], and in his

Historia Provinciae Anglicanae Societatis Iesu (St. Omers, 1660) the Jesuit Henry More praised him as 'conficiendarum domesticarum latebrarum peritissimus' ['most experienced in building domestic hiding places'; *my translation*].[36]

Life

Nicholas Owen was born into a devoutly Catholic family, the son of the carpenter Walter Owen, citizen of Oxford and one of four brothers. Two of the brothers were Jesuit priests, the third, Henry Owen, ran a covert Catholic printing press. Nicholas is likely to have been admitted into the Society of Jesus as a lay-brother about 1579 and served Father Edmund Campion on his first mission in 1580/81. He was briefly arrested in 1582 when he publicly proclaimed Campion's innocence, but was later released, because at that time, he was not a person in whom the Government would have seen a major threat. From 1588 he worked for Father Henry Garnet, the Mission's Superior. In 1594 Owen was briefly imprisoned and tortured but later released. He resumed his work and is believed to have assisted in the escape of Jesuit Father Gerard from the Tower of London in 1597. About 1600, an accident with a horse resulted in a broken leg and caused major physical disability.[37]

The aftermath of the Gunpowder Plot[38] led to Owen's arrest in Hindlip House in Worcestershire (see below) in early 1606. He was brought to the Tower of London, where he died[39] of torture in the night of 1-2 March 1606.[40]. Despite the most severe tortures he kept the secrets of his hiding places from his executioners without betraying anybody. According to Henry More, he was buried within the Tower. Nicholas Owen was beatified in 1929 and canonised as one of the Forty Martyrs of England and Wales (among them also Edmund Campion and Robert Southwell) by Pope Paul VI on 25 October 1970.

Legacy

Nicholas Owen has become famous for his extraordinary building skills, and it is safe to say that he was *the* mastermind behind Jesuit priest holes.[41] He is worthy to be compared to Daedalus, the builder of the Minoan Labyrinth (see Virgil, *Aeneid* V, 588-591 and Ovid, *Metamorphoses*, VIII, 157-168).[42] Owen and his work are mentioned in two letters by the Jesuit Robert Garnet, written in 1596 and 1599. Garnet says that Owen 'has travelled through almost the entire kingdom and has made for Catholic priests (apart from Jesuits) hiding-places where they can shelter from the fury of the heretical searchers' (Hodgetts, 'Mille Meandris' 186). 'The first extended account of him was in Tanner's *Societas Iesu Militans*, which was published in Prague in 1675' (Hodgetts, 'Mille Meandris' 179). Father Gerard stated that Owen was building hides 'for seventeen or eighteen years' (1588-1606; Hodgetts, 'The Owens at Oxford' 415). These were mainly the years between the victory over the Armada (as well as John Gerard's[43] return to England) in 1588 and the Gunpowder Plot of 1606. The priest hole at Braddocks in which John Gerard was hidden during the search of 1-4 April 1594

> is the only one for which we have Gerard's explicit statement that Owen built it, the only one for which we have both a first-hand description of its use and the spy's report which led to the search, and the only one of Owen's for which there is documentary evidence of its date (which was Christmas 1592)...[44]

It is still not definitely clear how many hides Owen really built, since many of them may not have been discovered to date.

Owen's Mastery

Hiding places had become necessary with the early Jesuit mission in the later 1570s and early 1580s. In these years, however, priest holes were still ill-constructed, ill-ventilated and insecure. Thus, the lives of many priests were endangered or even lost due to poor provision for their hidden concealment from the authorities. Nicholas Owen was to change all that fundamentally.

The main problem with a priest hole is how to mask the entrance. Furthermore, no two hiding places should be built in the same way, because the discovery of one could lead to the discovery of others of the same type. Nicholas Owen was a master in creating various kinds of hiding places, such as sliding doors and hidden crawl spaces, trap doors in turrets and stairways, connecting them, for instance, with the mansion's sewer system (as we find it in Coughton Court; see below). What is more and what is particularly interesting in this context is that Owen was famous for his ability 'to think in three dimensions and to exploit (or contrive) changes of level and the twist of staircases to disorientate the searchers. At least some of these are in houses which can be linked to the Jesuits between 1588 and 1605' (Hodgetts, 'Mille Meandris' 183).

Hiding Places in the Midlands

'No other part of England is richer in hiding-places than Worcestershire and the adjoining counties' (Hodgetts, *Secret Hiding Places*, 75); however, in the following I will trace only[45] those in which Nicholas Owen has left the legacy of his extraordinary building skills.[46]

In Warwickshire, nine miles north-west of Stratford-upon-Avon, is Coughton Court,[47] still the family home of the Catholic Throckmorton family who have lived there since 1409.

> Sir Robert Throckmorton, who died in 1586, was a first cousin of Lord Vaux of Harrowden, and his sons-in-law included Sir Thomas Tresham (who had been brought up at Coughton) and Sir William Catesby, one of the Gun Powder Plot conspirators. His niece Elizabeth, daughter of his brother Sir Nicholas the ambassador, married Sir Walter Raleigh. There was already a flourishing Mass centre at Coughton in the 1570s, as we learn from a Latin panegyric written by Southwell in honour of Edward Throckmorton, Sir Robert's nephew, who died as a student at the English college in Rome in 1582. ... an intercepted letter of April 1582, now among the State Papers, included commendations from Southwell in Rome to Robert Throckmorton at Coughton. (Hodgetts, *Secret Hiding Places*, 37)

When the Gunpowder Plot failed, 'the chief conspirators fled. Catesby with others made their way to Coughton. ... Garnett stayed at Coughton until 4th December when he and Anne Vaux went to Hinlip [sic] Castle, the seat of Sir Thomas Abington, ten miles out of Worcester, where Fr. Oldcorne had been living for twelve years'.[48]

With respect to Nicholas Owen, to date, Coughton Court represents a most fascinating site of his mastery:

> A hiding-place which probably existed at the time of the 1593 search can still be seen at Coughton. In the north-east corner of the Tower Room (the former secret chapel) is a small closet inside a hexagonal turret. The *floor* [my italics] of it is of modern boards, with a hole in the middle. Beneath is a secret compartment 4ft 1 in high and 4ft by 3ft 10ins at its widest. This also has a *floor* [my italics] of modern boards, under which again, is a lower secret compartment, the same shape and size as the upper one and 6ft 3ins high. When it was found in September 1858, it contained a rope ladder, a palliasse, three altar stones and a small piece of coarse tapestry in faded blue and yellow which is now on show in the Tower Room. The floor of this lower hole is made of four solid baulks of oak, each 5 ¼ins thick. One of these is movable, and below again is a newel staircase, blocked out 1780 when the present Great Staircase was built on the other side of the gatehouse but still with glazed windows.... (Hodgetts, *Secret Hiding Places*, 38)

Besides Coughton Court, Harvington Hall[49] in Worcestershire contains 'the most remarkable collection of hiding-places under one roof'.[50] Outwardly the mansion seems unremarkable, but inside it is one of the most complex and brilliant examples of priest holes that Owen ever devised. The house ceased to be used as a family house in 1696, and from then on, apart from occasional visits by the Throckmorton family (see above), it was occupied only by bailiffs, tenants and chaplains. By the 19th century it was so much neglected that it was to be dismantled. In 1910, Sir William Throckmorton removed the original staircase to Coughton. When in the 1930s restorations were begun by the present owners, that is, the Roman Catholic Archdiocese of Birmingham, 'the two previous centuries of suspended animation and neglect had ensured the survival of the hides, together with a remarkable series of wall-paintings, which were found under layers of whitewash in 1936' (Hodgetts, *Secret Hinding Places*, 85). There are no fewer than eight hiding places still to be seen today (in addition to the Nine Worthies Passage in the south-west wing). 'The suggestion that the hides at Harvington, or some of them, were the work of Nicholas Owen was first made in 1903 [and] there is now no reason to doubt the attribution ... and their close association with the Great Staircase would suggest a date between 1600 and 1605, towards the end of Owen's hide-building. (Hodgetts, *Secret Hiding Places*, 97)

John Habington, treasurer of Queen Elizabeth I's household, was recognized as the builder of another famous hiding place, Hindlip House. After the Gunpowder Plot had been unravelled, his heir Thomas Habington was arrested, and Hindlip was retained by the Crown, who leased it to Sir John Dromond in 1607, then granted it to William Kynnesman in the same year. After a fire in 1814 the original manor had to be demolished.

Not long after the Gunpowder Plot, a Catholic writer described Hindlip House as 'the most famous house in England for entertainment of priests'.[51] 'Gerard says that it was exactly like a Jesuit house on the Continent' (Hodgetts, *Secret Hiding Places*, 72). Built of brick, with stone dressings and a tiled roof, the walls were diapered with black brickwork. There were four blocks, built around a courtyard of about 24 yards square.

The house experienced two distinct periods as a Catholic stronghold, that is, from 1582 to 1586 and from 1590 to 1606, separated by a period of four years, during which the Protestant Dorothy

Habington was mistress of the house. The first period ended when Edward Habington was executed for alleged complicity in the Babington Plot, and his brother Thomas was imprisoned in the Tower. The second period began when Edward Oldcorne converted Dorothy Habington and took up residence at Hindlip in February 1589-90. The priests who served at Hindlip are unusually well documented, and Nicholas Owen is said to have been called on to build hiding holes within the confines of the house: 'eleven secret corners and conveyances were found there during the great twelve-day search of 1606 which resulted in the arrests of Owen himself, the Jesuit superior Henry Garnet, Edward Oldcorne, and Oldcorne's servant Blessed Ralph Ashley. But it was demolished in 1814 and must be reconstructed from documents.' (Hodgetts, 'Mille Meandris' 178f.)

The culture of *Doppelbödigkeit* as *tertium comparationis*

The manifold discourses of illusion,[52] deceit, manipulation, uncertainties, doubts, disguise, doubleness, and ambiguity as well as – on the linguistic side – paradox[53] and pun have all long been present in the history of early modern criticism (e.g., the culture of contrariety in the Petrarchan love sonnet, and the metaphysical conceit), in Shakespeare criticism, and in religious studies. As to the latter, Jesuits' *aliases* were common means of concealing their true identity. Furthermore, the Jesuits were accused of being equivocators, i.e. deceiving by the doubleness of their words (famously resonating in the porter scene in *Macbeth* and also – less frequently quoted – in the gravediggers' scene in *Hamlet*).

Linguistic *Doppelbödigkeit*

Shakespeare's extreme verbal sophistication has long been known,[54] be it in its infinite metrical or a-metrical variety or the double-speaking characters such as Iago or Richard III.

Puns are certainly one, but perhaps not the strongest aspect in the field of linguistic *Doppelbödigkeit*. Puns have been classified as 'other',[55] as leading the reader into a labyrinth.[56] Interestingly for our context, puns have also been interpreted as full of subversive potential, since they subvert the one-to-one relation between signifier and signified and thus challenge the stability of the (linguistic) order and lastly expose the arbitrariness of Saussure's signification.

> In a pun, one signifier is attached to two or more signifieds; the word can mean two or more things. It is because it ambiguates meaning that the pun disturbs the system of communication by which meaning is conveyed from speaker to listener, and upon which, in Saussure's view, any human society depends. That is why the pun has traditionally been treated as an anarchist, as a *traitor* [my italics] who breaks rank with meaning. (Bates, 'The Point of Puns', 424)

Bates even finds an explicit (Catholic) religious dimension associated with the pun:

> Kept to the point as a discrete and bounded entity, the pun poses no problem to the serious critic. It is good. It exercises his ingenuity and expertise... But when the pun shifts from this position and begins to duck and to weave – to crop up in unexpected places, to elude the critic's grasp – then it is bad. The serious critic begins unnervingly to lose his grip. Meaning looks more and more *illusory* [my italics] – and not only in the literary text he is interpreting but, much more worryingly, in his own. He has been cheated and defrauded, handed an empty envelope. ... He may do all he can to overcome this. ... But the repressed always returns. And the bad pun – that lightest of words – is like a ghost which can never be put to rest but which will keep on coming back from *purgatory* [my italics] to haunt him. (Bates, 'The Point of Puns', 438)

Visual *Doppelbödigkeit: trompe l'oeil and anamorphosis*

For our Jesuit context, I will now introduce two hitherto neglected phenomena to the discussion in which the culture of *Doppelbödigkeit* appears to be extremely well represented, i.e., trompe l'oeil and anamorphosis.

Trompe l'oeil (French for 'deceive the eye'), also known as illusion painting, is an artistic technique creating the optical illusion that the depicted objects appear in three dimensions. The phrase goes back to the Baroque period, when it was used in order to refer to perspectival illusionism. What is decisive for us is that the mannerist and Baroque style interiors of Jesuit churches in the 16th and 17th centuries often included trompe l'oeil paintings which open up the ceiling or dome to the heavens. The most prominent artist of the Society may be Andrea Pozzo (1642-1709), a master of illusionistic painting style, which is most spectacularly demonstrated on the ceiling of the church of Sant' Ignazio in Rome (1691-94). Pozzo has particularly been celebrated as an artist who draws a spectator into an artistic performance and encourage him to actively engage with paintings and architecture. What is more, Emperor Rudolph II of Prague was an ardent collector of trompe l'oeil paintings and curiosities.[57]

Besides trompe l'oeil, anamorphosis (Greek for 'formed again') as another realisation of *Doppelbödigkeit* is a distorted projection or perspective requiring the view to use special devices or occupy a specific vantage point to reconstruct the image. Anamorphic painting thus consists of the paradoxes of distorting perspectives. Baltruasitis has stressed the intellectual power in the visual paradoxes that are anamorphic paintings: 'The system was established as a technical curiosity, but it embraces a poetry of abstraction, an effective mechanism for producing optical illusion and a philosophy of false reality. It is an enigma, a wonder, a marvel.'[58] The best-known example may be Hans Holbein the Younger's painting *The Ambassadors*, in which a seemingly distorted shape or enigmatic disk lies diagonally across the bottom of the frame. Viewing it from an acute angle, however, transforms it into the plastic image of a *memento mori* skull.

Nicholas Owen and the culture of *Doppelbödigkeit*

As indicated above, Nicholas Owen's priest holes were the marvels of the time.

> Hides that can be ascribed to Owen are often towards the centre of the house, which means they cannot be located by walking round outside; and they show evidence of thinking in three dimensions. At ... several ... houses, brilliant use is made of staircases next to hides: the searcher cannot stand still and keep his sense of direction. This three-dimensional dynamic planning to create an *illusion* [my italics] is commonly credited to Baroque architects of the 17th century but it has other uses as well. Where Owen burrowed into masonry or brickwork, it was in consequence of his liking for sites away from outside walls, where the main structure of the house could be exploited, not just projections from it. ... The Harvington hide was originally double, is not burrowed out of stone or brickwork, had no emergency exit, and is at the junction of two spiral staircases (curving in opposite directions) and a short straight one.[59]

What is more in our field of *Doppelbödigkeit* is the concrete dimension of two *Böden* (in the sense of two 'floors'). As indicated above, some of the places Owen built were concealed inside another hidden room in order to divert the government's priest-hunters' attention from the main priest hide. A brilliant example of such a-matter-of-fact *Doppelbödigkeit* can be seen at Harvington Hall, where the hide below the top landing of the Great Staircase has a space for valuables, which in turn hides the entrance to the priest-hide itself.

William Shakespeare and the culture of *Doppelbödigkeit*

With regard to Shakespeare, surprisingly little appears to have been done in the particular fields of trompe l'oeil and anamorphosis. Catherine Belsey's essay on trompe l'oeil[60] follows Lacan's (very special) definition.[61] Belsey sees trompe l'oeil in a rather generalized way as a 'lack of closure' (258)[62] and is mostly concerned with signifiers of (evading) desire and gender roles in the poem. Her approach differs widely from my interdisciplinary approach to trompe l'oeil.

As to anamorphosis, one of the few who have acknowledged this very phenomenon is Gustav René Hocke in his interpretation of Juliet's mourning over Romeo's body. He sees her speech as 'doubled' by grief and thus spatially resembling the frescoes by Federico Zuccari.[63]

Richard II

For the final part of this article, I will have a closer look at selected texts throughout Shakespeare's career that can be linked with the idea of anamorphosis. In all cases, in moments of astonishment, surprise or even shock, the speaking characters allude to anamorphic painting in which – as outlined above – one thing can possess two discrete realities, depending on the viewer's perspective. Rather early in Shakespeare's career, in *Richard II*, Bushy tries to comfort the Queen as follows:

> Each substance of a grief hath twenty shadows,
> Which shows like grief itself, but is not so.   15
> For sorrow's eye, glazed with blinding tears,
> Divides one thing entire to many objects,
> Like perspectives, which, rightly gaz'd upon,
> Show nothing but confusion; ey'd awry,
> Distinguish form. So your sweet Majesty,   20
> Looking awry upon your Lord's departure
> Find shapes of grief more than himself to wail,
> Which, looked on as it is, is nought but shadows
> Of what it is not; then, thrice-gracious queen,
> More than your Lord's departure weep not – more's not seen,   25
> Or if it be, 'tis with false sorrow's eye,
> Which, for things true, weeps things imaginary. (2.2.14-27)[64]

Besides *Richard II*, in *Twelfth Night*, Orsino, upon seeing the twins Viola and Sebastian, exclaims: 'One face, one voice, one habit, and two persons, / A natural perspective that is and is not' (5.1.208-09). This passage is echoed by Troilus' insight that 'this is and is not Cressid' (*Troilus and Cressida*, 5.2.146).

Antony and Cleopatra

In *Antony and Cleopatra* (2.5.117-118),[65] the latter bids her ladies in waiting to find out as much as possible about Antony's new Roman wife:

Go to the fellow, good Alexas, bid him	112
Report the feature of Octavia; her years,	
Her inclination, let him not leave out	
The colour of her hair. Bring me word quickly.	115
Let him for ever go, let him not, Charmian,	
Though he be painted one way like a Gorgon	
The other way's a Mars.	118

As these quotations suggest, the dramatist and poet William Shakespeare thus appears to have not only been familiar with the techniques of (theatrical) illusion and linguistic doubleness as such but also with the visual paradox of anamorphosis – which indeed was highly popular in the paintings of Jesuit churches and the technique of building of priest holes by Nicholas Owen.

The Winter's Tale

As to doubleness of illusion in general, I should like to conclude this section with a brief reference to the revival of Hermione's statue in *The Winter's Tale*. In Shakespeare's source, Greene's *Pandosto*, the accused queen Bellaria dies, but Shakespeare employs a most powerful theatrical device by having her statue revived. The decisive argument with reference to *Doppelbödigkeit*, however, is that the privilege of discrepant awareness is denied to the audience.[66] Hermione being alive and only hidden away by Emilia remains concealed to them as well as to the characters on stage. The audience thus – to my knowledge uniquely in Shakespeare's complete works – remain in their 'double' perspective, sharing the perspective of the characters and also watching the play as a whole.

Conclusion

It has been the aim of this article to throw some light on the inextricable relationship between the Jesuits and the British Bard, and to suggest a *tertium comparationis* between William Shakespeare and the religious context of the early Jesuit mission. I have tried to show that Shakespeare's most enigmatic biography cannot only be further explored and enriched by more historical documents – which are unlikely to be found – but also by more abstract concepts and cultural discourses of the early modern period. The general idea of creating various forms of illusion, be it in the theatre or by building (three- dimensional) priest holes, is a case in point. As it turned out, the German term *Doppelbödigkeit* might be most appropriate as a *tertium comparationis*, since it includes the concrete idea of 'two floors' as, for instance, realised in the double priest hole in Harvington Hall, but also the figurative sense of double meaning. What is more, from an interdisciplinary approach, the visual techniques of trompe l'oeil and anamorphosis proved most fruitful conceptual frameworks for an array of various perspectives, be it in the field of literature or (Jesuit) architecture. The master builder of priest holes, Nicholas Owen, handled space in order to create an illusion which was worthy of a Baroque architect, even if his materials were less refined and his purpose much more serious. For his priest hides, he used trompe l'oeil perspective and many of the modern principles of illusionistic stage design. *Vice versa*, the master of theatrical and verbal illusion, William Shakespeare, was a master of visual illusion such as anamorphosis.[67]

All in all, I would hope to have shed light on a previously underexplored topic, and there is much work still to be done. It seems that the study of the visual arts in an early modern religious context cries out for an interdisciplinary research agenda, that is, art historians working alongside literary critics.

Sonja Fielitz is Full Professor of English Literature at the University of Marburg (Germany). She studied English, Latin and German at the University of Munich and received her PhD in 1992 with a study on Shakespeare's *Timon of Athens* and its relation to a hitherto unknown *Timon* play by the German Jesuit Jakob Gretser. Her postdoctoral thesis, published in 2000, examines the status of Ovid's

Metamorphoses within the various theoretical and critical discourses in England between 1660 and 1800. She is (board) member of numerous academic organisations and has published widely on the early modern period with a focus on Shakespeare and contemporaries, the long eighteenth century, children's literature, and modern drama and film.

Notes

1. I dedicate this article to Professor Dr. Wolfgang Weiss (1932 – 2019) in grateful memory.
2. Other than Catholics, Protestants assert the supremacy of religious sound – God's word made audible in preaching – over the (in their view) idolatrous deceptions of the sight directed to the elevation of the Eucharistic host at Catholic Mass, to pictures and statutes of Christ and the saints, and to miracles.
3. Further reading suggestions on Jesuit architecture include: Konrad A. Ottenheym, Krista De Jonge and Monique Chatenet (eds.), *Public Buildings in Modern Europe* (Turnhout: Brepols, 2010); Richard Bösel, *Jesuitenarchitektur in Italien (1540-1773)* (Vienna: Österreichische Akademie der Wissenschaften, 2007); Idem, "Grundsatzfragen und Fallstudien zur Jesuitischen Bautypologie". In: Werner Telesko and Herbert Karner (eds.), *Die Jesuiten in Wien: Zur Kunst- und Kulturgeschichte der Österreichischen Ordensprovinz der Gesellschaft im 17. und 18. Jahrhundert* (Vienna: Österreichische Akademie der Wissenschaften, 2003). Idem, "Typus und Tradition in der Baukultur gegenreformatorischer Orden", *Römische historische Mitteilungen* 31 (1989), 239-253.
4. A German term for which there appears to exist no exact equivalent in English. According to my British colleagues, the best literal translation would be 'hulled', which is, however, uncommon in literary contexts. The German word is so appropriate because *Boden* (in -*bödig*-) implies the real dimension of 'floor' but also the figural dimension of 'doubleness' / 'having two layers (of meaning)'. In his *Shakespeare und die Tradition des Volkstheaters* (Berlin: Henschel, 1975), the late Robert Weimann also uses the term *Doppelbödigkeit* (121ff). The English translation of his study (which, however, is much more a heavily revised and abridged adaptation!), edited by Robert Schwartz (Baltimore/ London: Johns Hopkins University Press, 1978) renders the adjective *doppelbödig* – incorrectly – by 'flexible' (73). Elsewhere on the same page Schwartz uses the term 'doubleness' (73; again on 77f). On page 85 he even reproduces Weimann's *Mehrbödigkeit* as 'dramaturgy'!
5. See, for instance, John Klause, *Shakespeare, the Earl, and the Jesuit* (Cranbury NJ: Rosemont, 2008). The Jesuit featuring in the title is Robert Southwell, whose work, Klause argues, Shakespeare must have known, remembering its most striking passages in detail. See for this footnote: F.W. Brownlow's review of Klause's study in *Shakespeare Quarterly* 61.1 (2010): 132-34.
6. Quoted in: J.E. Neale, *Elizabeth I and Her Parliaments, 1584-1601* (1958; New York: Norton, 1966), p. 424.
7. David Scott Kastan. *A Will to Believe. Shakespeare and Religion* (Oxford: Oxford University Press, 2014), p. 3.
8. Christopher Baker, *Religion in the Age of Shakespeare* (Westport, CT: Greenwood Press, 2007); Jonathan Dollimore and Terry Eagleton, *Radical Tragedy: Religion,*

Ideology and Power in the Drama of Shakespeare and his Contemporaries (Basingstoke: Palgrave Macmillan, 2004); Stephen Greenblatt, *Renaissance Self-Fashioning: From More to Shakespeare* (Chicago: University of Chicago Press, 1980); *Hamlet in Purgatory* (Princeton: Princeton University Press, 2001); Gary Taylor, '"Forms of Opposition": Shakespeare and Middleton', *English Literary Renaissance* 24 (1994): 283-314; Alexandra Walsham, *Charitable Hatred: Tolerance and Intolerance in England 1500-1700* (Manchester: Manchester University Press, 2006).

9. June Schlueter and Dennis McCarthy, *'A brief Discourse of Rebellion and Revels' by George North. A newly uncovered manuscript source for Shakespeare's Plays* (Cambridge: D. S. Brewer, 2018). Review by Andrea Campana, "All Roads Lead to Campion": George North, William Shakespeare, and the Chandos Portrait", *The Heythrop Journal* LX (2019), 170-196.

10. Ernst Anselm Joachim Honigmann, *Shakespeare: The Lost Years* (Manchester: Manchester University Press, 1985; 1998).

11. Peter Milward, *Shakespeare's Religious Background* (Bloomington and London: Indiana University Press, 1973); Anthony Holden; *William Shakespeare: His Life and Work* (London: Little, Brown and Company, 1999).

12. See, for instance, Robert Bearman, '"Was William Shakespeare William Shakeshafte" Revisited', *Shakespeare Quarterly* 53 (2002): 83-94.

13. Gerard Kilroy, *Edmund Campion: Memory and Transcription* (London: Ashgate, 2006); Arthur F. Marotti (ed.), *Catholicism and Anti-Catholicism in Early Modern English Texts* (Basingstoke: Macmillan; New York: St. Martin's Press, 1999); Idem, *Religious Ideology and Cultural Fantasy: Catholic and anti-Catholic discourses in early modern England* (Notre Dame, Indiana: Notre Dame University Press, 2009); Thomas McCoog, S.J., *Monumenta Anglia: English and Welsh Jesuits: Catalogues (1555-1629)*, 2 vols (Rome, Institutum Historicum Societas Iesu, 1992); Alison Shell, *Catholicism, Controversy and the English Literary Imagination, 1558-1660* (Cambridge: Cambridge University Press, 1999); 'Why didn't Shakespeare write religious verse?' in: Takashi Kozuka and J.R. Mulryne (eds), *Shakespeare, Marlowe, Jonson: New Directions in Biography* (Burlington, VT: Ashgate, 2006), 85-112; Paul Whitfield White, *Drama and Religion in English Provincial Society, 1485-1660* (Cambridge: Cambridge University Press, 2008).

14. Wilson appropriates the topic for a distinctly dissident Shakespeare. See, for instance, his *Secret Shakespeare: Studies in Theatre, Religion and Resistance* (Manchester: Manchester University Press, 2004), and '"Blood Will Have Blood": Regime Changes in *Macbeth*', *Shakespeare Jahrbuch* 143 (2007): 11-35. See also Richard Dutton, Alison Findlay, Richard Wilson (eds.), *Theatre and Religion: Lancastrian Shakespeare*, 2 vols (Manchester: Manchester University Press, 2003), including my own 'Learned Pate and Golden Fool: A Jesuit source for Shakespeare's *Timon of Athens*', 179-96.

15. Thomas Alfred, *Shakespeare, Catholicism, and the Middle Ages* (London: Palgrave Macmillan, 2018); Lowell Gallagher (ed.), *Redrawing the Map of Early Modern English Catholicism* (Toronto: University of Toronto Press, 2012); Peter Iver Kaufmann, *Religion Around Shakespeare* (Penn State University Press, 2013); James E. Kelly and Susan Royal (eds.), *Early Modern English Catholicism - Identity, Memory and Counter-Reformation* (Leiden: Brill, 2016).

16. Thomas McCoog SJ, *Pre-suppression. Jesuit Activity in the British Isles and Ireland* (Leiden: Brill, 2019).

17. Ginevra Crosignani, Thomas McCoog, Michael Questier (eds.), *Recusancy and Conformity in Early Modern England: Manuscript and Printed Sources in Translation* (Toronto: Pontifical Institute of Medieval Studies, 2010).

18. Graham Holderness, Katherine Scheil (eds.), *Critical Survey*, 21.3 (2009), including my own 'Shakespeare and Catholicism: The Jesuits as Cultural Mediators in Early Modern Europe': 54-68.
19. See, for instance, John C.H. Aveling, *The Handle and the Axe: The Catholic Recusants in England from Reformation to Emancipation* (London: Bond and Briggs, 1976); John Bossy, *The English Catholic Community 1570-1850* (New York: Oxford University Press, 1976).
20. For Shakespeare's biography against a Catholic background, see: Clare Asquith, 'The Catholic Bard: Shakespeare and the "Old Religion"'. *Commonweal* 132.12 (2005): 10-14; Dympna Callaghan, 'Shakespeare and Religion', *Textual Practice* 15.1 (2001): 1-4.
21. Michael Hodgetts, *Secret Hiding Places* (Dublin: Veritas Publications, 1989), 81.
22. S.P. 12/243/76, f. 239, quoted by Michael Hodgetts, 'Elizabethan Priest-Holes III', *Recusant History*, 12.1 (1973): 171-97, 182.
23. On his religious belief, see, for instance, Robert Bearman, 'John Shakespeare: A Papist or Just Penniless?', *Shakespeare Quarterly* 56.4 (2005): 411-33.
24. See, for instance, Velma Bourgeois Richmond, *Shakespeare, Catholicism, and Romance* (New York and London: Continuum, 2000), 81-83.
25. E.g., Robert N. Watson, '*Othello* as a Reformation Tragedy', in Thomas Moisan and Douglas Bruster (eds.), *In the Company of Shakespeare* (London: Associated University Presses, 2002), 65-96; Tom Bishop, 'The Burning Hand: Poetry and Reformation in Shakespeare's *Richard II*'. *Religion and Literature* 32.2 (2000): 29-47; John Klause, 'Catholic and Protestant, Jesuit and Jew: Historical Religion in *The Merchant of Venice*'. *Religion and the Arts* 7.1-2 (2003): 65-102; Helen Wilcox, 'Shakespeare's Miracle Play? Religion in *All's Well that Ends Well*', in: Gary Waller (ed.), *All's Well that Ends Well: New Critical Essays* (New York: Routledge, 2007), 140-54.
26. On September 27, 1540 Pope Paul III (1468-1549) approved the establishment of the Society of Jesus with the bull "Regimini militantis ecclesiae", and the Society was dissolved in 1773 by Pope Clement XIV with the publication of the brief "Dominus ac Redemptor noster", and restored in 1814. The Jesuits became the main instrument of the Counter-Reformation, and the purpose of the Society was the propagation and strengthening of the Catholic faith everywhere in the world. See Thomas Banchoff and José Casanova (eds.), *The Jesuits and Globalization: Historical Legacies and Contemporary Challenges* (Washington DC: Georgetown University Press, 2016); McCoog, Thomas SJ (ed), *With Eyes and Ears Open: The Role of Visitors in the Society of Jesus* (Leiden: Brill, 2019).
27. For instance, emblems. See Peter M. Daly and G. Richard Dimler S.J., *The Jesuit Emblem in the European Context* (Philadelphia, PA: Saint Joseph's University Press 2016).
28. For recent contributions to Jesuit visual arts, see S. Clark, *Vanities of the Eye: Vision in Early Modern European Culture* (Oxford, 2007); Ralph DeKoninck, *Ad Imaginem. Statuts, fonctions, and usages de l'image dans la littérature spirituelle jésuite du XVII sciècle* (Geneva: Droz, 2005); Alison Fleming, "Images", in *The Cambridge Encyclopedia of the Jesuits*, ed. Thomas Worcester (Cambridge: Cambridge University Press, 2017), 378-384; Wietse de Boer, Karl A. Enekel, and Walter S. Melion (eds.), *Jesuit Image Theory* (Leiden: Brill, 2016); Elisabeth Oy-Marra and Volker Remmert (eds.), *Le monde est une peinture: Jesuitische Identität und die Rolle der Bilder* (Berlin: Akdadmie Verlag, 2011); John W. O'Malley (ed.), *Art, Controversy, and the Jesuits: The Imago primi saeculi* (16140), (Philadelphia, PA: Saint Joseph's University Press

2015); Alan Tapié (ed.), *Baroque Vision Jésuite: Du Tintoretto a Rubens* (Paris: Somogy éditions d'Art, 2003).
29. In the field of rhetoric, orators were encouraged to deploy a wide spectrum of image-based tropes in defence of the faith. 'The order of the Jesuits often evokes the *imago* and its species such as *figura, pictura, repraesentatio, similitudo, simulacrum, speculum* in order to celebrate 'the Deus Artifex who fashioned Jesus Christ, the divinely human imago Dei, and thereby translated his incarnate person and Holy Name into imagines newly discernible to human senses, heart, and minds.' Wietse de Boer, "Introduction", in: Wietse de Boer, Karl A. Enekel, and Walter S. Melion (eds.), *Jesuit Image Theory* (Leiden: Brill, 2016), 4.
30. Wietse de Boer, "Introduction", 8.
31. On religion and the senses, see Wietse de Boer, C. Göttler (eds.), *Religion and the Senses in Early Modern Europe* (Leiden: Brill, 2013); Jeffrey Chipps Smith, *Sensuous Worship: Jesuits and the Art of the Early Catholic Reformation in Germany* (Princeton: Princeton University Press, 2002).
32. Alison C. Fleming, "Jesuit Visual Culture: Communication, Globalization, and Relationships", *Journal of Jesuit Studies* 6 (2019), 187-195, at 187.
33. Alison C. Fleming, "Jesuit Visual Culture", 188.
34. Even in Jesuit studies, Nicholas Owen has long been neglected: '[u]ntil recently, interest in martyrs dominated the field. Their biographies, i.e., of Edmund Campion, Robert Southwell, Henry Garnet, were written but important men such as Robert Parsons and Richard Blunt, first provincial in England, were ignored.' Thomas M. McCoog, *The Society of Jesus in Ireland, Scotland, and England 1541-1588: 'Our Way of Proceeding'* (Leiden, New York and Köln: Brill, 1996), 6. *The Cambridge Encyclopedia of the Jesuits*, general editor Thomas Worcester SJ (Cambridge: Cambridge University Press, 2017) does not list Nicholas Owen.
35. A priest hole is usually an almost featureless space, identifiable by its secret entrance.
36. Quoted in Michael Hodgetts, 'Mille Meandris', *Recusant History* 28.2 (2006): 189 note 1.
37. See Michael Hodgetts, 'The Owens of Oxford', *Recusant History* 24.4 (1999): 415-30; 417.
38. See, for instance, Antonia Fraser, *The Gunpowder Plot: Terror and Faith in 1605* (London: Weidenfeld & Nicolson, 1996).
39. For the description of his death see: http://stnicholasowen.co.uk.
40. 'It was given out that he had committed suicide with a table-knife, and a ballad with a woodcut illustration was printed to encourage this rumour' (Hodgetts, *Secret Hiding Places*, 179)
41. Less than a hundred houses still contain known hides. Many recusants and castles were damaged during the Civil War and either reconstructed afterwards, like Coughton Court, or abandoned altogether. Even in houses that survived, hiding-places may have been altered and destroyed over the centuries.
42. '... a few hides below ground are recorded: at Baddesley Clinton in Warwickshire, and the Blackfriar's Gatehouse in London.' Hodgetts, 'Mille Meandris', 189 n15.
43. For Owen's arrest and praise of his work see John Gerard, *Narrative of the Gunpowder Plot*, quoted in Michael Hodgetts, 'Elizabethan Priest Holes: I – Dating and Chronology', *Recusant History*, 11.6 (1972): 284f..
44. 'In the Oxford D.N.B. I listed only six houses which contain surviving hides by him: in their probably chronological order: Oxburgh, Baddesley Clinton, Braddocks, Sawston, Scotney, Harvington.' Hodgetts, 'Mille Meandris', 182.

45. 'Six miles north-west of Harleyford across the Chilterns, and four miles north of Henley-on-Thames, is Stonor, one of the most notable recusant houses in England. (Hodgetts, *Secret* 33).
46. At Stonor, Campion and Persons had their headquarters from April to July 1581, and here Campion's *Decem Rationes* (*Ten Reasons*) was printed on a secret press. ... At the end of June, Fr William Hartley, a former Fellow of St. John's, smuggled copies of Campion's book into Oxford and left them on the benches in the University church before the Commencement ceremony. On 11 July, Persons and Campion rode away from Stonor together and parted for the last time on the common. Less than a week later, on 17 July, Campion was arrested at Lyford' (Hodgetts, *Secret* 33).
47. Apart from its priest-holes, Coughton Court is also fascinating due to the so-called *Tabula Eliensis*, 'a huge painted cloth which now hangs in the Tower Room. It has been dated to 1596, and it depicts Ely Cathedral with its spire, together with portraits of all the sovereigns from William the Conqueror to Elizabeth and the arms of all the Catholic gentry who were imprisoned during her reign, grouped under their various places of imprisonment.' Hodgetts, *Secret Hiding Places*, 42.
48. Ethelred L. Taunton, *The History of the Jesuits in England 1580-1773* (London: Methuen & Co, 1901), 301f..
49. I am most grateful to Rev. Dr. Paul Edmondson who kindly recommended Harvington Hall for my first visit. For literature on it, see Hodgetts, *Secret Hiding Places*, 82-99 and Michael Hodgetts, 'Elizabethan Priest Holes: IV – Harvington', *Recusant History*, 13.1 (1975): 18-55.
50. Granville Squiers, *Secret Hiding Places* (London, 1933). Quoted in Hodgetts, 'Priest Holes IV', 18.
51. Hodgetts, 'Elizabethan Priest-Holes III', 184. Hodgetts refers to 130:SO 881586, according to Foley 4, 213-16. Also found in Hodgetts, 'Mille Meandris', 178f.
52. See, for instance, Anthony B. Dawson, *Indirections: Shakespeare and the Art of Illusion* (Toronto, Buffalo and London: University of Toronto Press, 1978).
53. See Peter G. Platt, *Shakespeare and the Culture of Paradox* (London: Ashgate, 2009). For further titles in this field, see Platt, 45, n 91. Platt in his very substantial study of paradox does not tie in with the field of religious studies.
54. 'Dabei geht Shakespeare mit dem Gebrauch von Sprichwort, Wortspiel und Metapher viel weiter als etwa Marlowe oder Kyd'. Weimann, 347. This passage is omitted in the English adaptation ed. by Robert Schwartz.
55. 'The pun is marked as other and derives its status as such from being measured against an everyday, sober method of expression treated as the norm'. Catherine Bates, 'The Point of Puns', *Modern Philology* 96.4 (1999), 421-438, at 425.
56. 'In Eco's view, bad puns are too ambiguous ... if defined any more loosely, the pun would ultimately threaten to lead the critic off into a labyrinth of totally unrelated associations'. Bates, 431.
57. See Eckhardt Hollmann, Jürgen Tesch, *Die Kunst der Augentäuschung* (München: Prestel, 2004), 13.
58. Baltrusaitis, *Anamorphic Art*, 1. Quoted in Platt, 27.
59. Hodgetts, 'Elizabethan Priest Holes: I – Dating and Chronology', 290.
60. 'Love as Trompe-l'oeil: Taxonomies of Desire in *Venus and Adonis*', *Shakespeare Quarterly* 46.3 (1995), 257-76.
61. Patricia Dorval's essay 'Gazing through the Peephole of Rhetoric: Shakespearean Trompe L'oeil Then and Now', *Cahiers Elisabéthains* 51 (1972): 63-75 subsumes almost anything under the term *trompe l'oeil* and is fairly incomprehensible.

62. 'A literal trompe l'oeil, a text of and about desire, *Venus and Adonis* promises a definite account of love but at the same time withholds the finality that such a promise might lead us to expect'.
63. 'Das Wortspiel steigert, in einem Augenblick derart persönlicher Erregung, die Metapher aus bloß sinnlichen Bezügen in raumsprengede Doppeldeutigkeit. Der Wahn der Trauer wird doppelt sichtbar, so wie Figuren in Decken-Fresken Federico Zuccaris sich mit dem wandernden Betrachter auf ihn zubewegen oder sich von ihm entfernen' Gustav René Hocke, *Manierismus in der Literatur: Sprach-Alchimie und esoterische Kombinationskunst* (Hamburg: Rowohlt, 1959), 94.
64. Both the New Cambridge Shakespeare Edition (ed. Andrew Gurr), and the Arden Edition (ed. Peter Ure) refer to anamorphosis for these lines.
65. The footnote in the Arden Edition by M.R. Ridley, does not see (as I do) anamorphosis here but rather 'two objects that are painted on the opposite sides of any suitable material ... which is then cut into regular strips and attached to a third painted surface at small equal intervals, and at right angles to it' (75).
66. See Ingeborg Boltz (ed.), *The Winter's Tale. Das Wintermärchen* (Tübingen: Francke, 1986), 346, fn 3.
67. Last but not least, William Shakespeare and Nicholas Owen have both been turned into fictional characters. Nicholas Owen (however, incorrectly named Hugh Owen) features in Robert Hugh Benson's novel *Came Back! Come Rope!* (1912), and one of Owen's double priest holes plays a key role in Catherine Aird's detective novel *A Most Contagious Game* (1967). But this would be a different story, and a different essay altogether.

Chapter 4
To Change the Picture of Shakespeare Biography

Park Honan

A report on my experience with *Shakespeare: A Life* may not be generally useful, but I shall touch on factors that are changing our view of literary biography. It helps to refer to oneself and to the matter of a biographer's outlook and feelings, no matter how deplorable the feelings. Of course, what a biographer thinks or feels is irrelevant, in one sense. We don't care what you may have felt, for heaven's sake; we judge your work! That is proper as far as it goes, but outlook and preparedness count in this field and so I shall allude to those. My general view is that biography thrives when we regard it as highly sophisticated, entertaining, and moving, and able to depict as much about life as works of fiction can. This genre has a certain relation to music and painting in its possible intensity. 'All that is not useful', says Matisse, 'is detrimental to the effect'; the same applies to biographical narratives. Shakespeare's life offers a special challenge, but not for any dire lack of evidence. Much depends on what use is made of abundant facts about Tudor Stratford, for example, and so on a personal attitude. My early attitude to Shakespeare was romantic and poor. For some time I thought of him as semi-divine, or as being 'more than a man'. If I liked 'Prufrock', that was for its *Hamlet* allusions mainly. Later at University College in London, I was taken aback when my supervisor asked me to read something besides Shakespeare before trying to write a PhD thesis on the tragedies. I wrote two plays, both staged by London groups, but reviewed harshly in student newspapers, except for a remark to the effect that 'Honan is incapable of writing anything but duologues, rather like Shakespeare in *Two Gentlemen of Verona*'. Finally I wrote a thesis on Browning partly because 'Caliban upon Setebos' reminded me of *The Tempest*.

Having a crush on an author can increase one's impatience with existing works on the figure. After beginning to teach, I found Shakespeare biographies below par, but beyond my scope. I did finish a life of Browning on request, and later wrote lives of Arnold and of Jane Austen. These were odd topics for a Shakespeare addict, but a biographer is led to think of genre and form, and that was helpful. At the time literary biography had experienced a great flourishing, which began in the 1950s and resulted in works such as Richard Ellmann's *Joyce*, L.A. Marchand's *Byron*, and Gordon N. Ray's *Thackeray*; fifty years on no better lives of those subjects have appeared, which is not to say that biography has floundered hopelessly ever since. Edel's *Henry James* and Painter's *Proust* also belong initially to the time. All of these works were partly inspired by T.S. Eliot and the New Criticism's emphasis on the opus – the created poem, play, or novel which was thought to be autotelic and self-sufficient, a thing to be criticized on its own, as if independent of the author. Still there was a corollary, which Eliot had described very well in 'Ben Jonson' (1919) in saying that the making of a stage-character 'consists in the process of the transfusion of the personality, or, in a deeper sense, the life, of the author into the character' and that the ways of this authorial transfusion are 'complex and devious'. This gave a formula for literary biography, which might show how Ben Jonson or Keats developed and what became transfused into their works, except that the theory neglected broad as well as specific social contexts.

With the last matter in view, let me allude to Ray, Ellmann, and Schoenbaum. I have kept a writer's diary called 'Festina Lente' since the age of twenty-one, and in this there is a reference to a final meeting with Gordon N. Ray, at the Athenaeum Club, in June 1986. Ray looked like Thackeray; he was then overweight and trembly, an elephantine man with a cherubic face, unlikely to be capable of revisiting London, but glad to reminisce. 'Did you have any particular biographical model in mind for your *Thackeray*?', I asked. 'No', said Ray, 'I looked around but couldn't find any models for what I wanted to do. I aimed to do a social model of the times, using Thackeray as an archetype of the writer'. He and Ellmann both recognized, I think, that narrow biographical forms had failed to accommodate 'social models' or adequate treatments of social history in close specific relation to an author. Ray and Ellmann respectively with Thackeray and Joyce did get around difficulty; but Shakespeare's biographers had not done so, and instead relied on loosely attached or fancifully evocative paragraphs of 'background', or, as in Samuel Schoenbaum's *Documentary Life*, they skimped on social contexts, though that work achieves other ends. In Washington DC, I met Schoenbaum and found him alert to the problem. He was most helpful, always modestly encouraging criticism; we talked as if we were graduate students. Only ill health kept him from writing a contextualized biography of the playwright that he had planned. But, sadly, it didn't exist.

When I began my life of Shakespeare, the problem of related contexts seemed difficult, delicate, but essential to deal with. French structural historians of the Annales school such as Fernand Braudel explored society's effects upon the individual in new ways; our methods of representing anyone's life in the distant past looked outdated, though I never became a disciple of Braudel especially. It seemed necessary to work out my own approaches to form, as I tried to do in *Authors' Lives* (1990). But why was the social problem difficult? I aimed to write a full, factual, scholarly biography adding to the tradition of Malone, Halliwell-Phillipps, Fripp, Chambers, and Schoenbaum, but this depended upon using a continuous narrative, in order to separate fact from supposition. I needed to avoid the retrospective fallacy, a darting back to suggest this or that about an Elizabethan. Only by keeping a sense of the subject in view in an evolving 'historical present' can one hope to avoid falsity with a topic as difficult as the creative mind. Ellmann achieves continuity in *Joyce*, and has Joyce's letters to offset the disrupting intrusion of passages about locale, history, or broad context. Diaries and letters by Arnold, and those by the Austens helped to keep subjects 'on the page' or in view. Such help, of course, is lacking for a life of Marlowe or Shakespeare, but did not inhibit me lately in writing *Christopher Marlowe: Poet & Spy* for which there was a considerable amount of new information to deal with, nor did it with Shakespeare. There has been a great feature in our advance in delicacy and pertinence since we have begun to recognize that 'social context' – a failing in lives of Shakespeare – can be used in support of factual and precise continuity.

I adopted several principles to help with the practice of *Shakespeare: A Life*, and hold to them as truthful. First, it should be considered that 'background' is never desirable in a biography. One may need to explain facts about Tudor London, such as that it was noisier than Stratford, that its need for grain was 11.5 per cent higher during the law terms, or that the Red Lion theatre had been built in a certain year. All of this represents what Shakespeare met with in London: a cacophony of church bells, 'termers' or law students in seasonal droves, or prefabricated theatres built years before he reached St Helen's parish. Sometimes one can be and should be excessively precise. Did he know exactly of 11.5 per cent rises in grain needs? Perhaps not, but theatre men benefited from the law-terms, and the figure quantifies what every city actor knew something about, so I used it. If one excludes the idea of mere 'background', it is possible to work with the real artistry of facts and relevance, or, for example to suffuse a sketch of Tudor London with a sense of one young poet's 'presence' while respecting hard evidence. Always diachronic narrative is in a weave with synchronic allusions and comment, so one has endless opportunities to keep an ongoing and changing sense of 'Shakespeare-in-London' in view. And just what is to be made of that? Well, my understanding of his growth or development was helped by research, but as much as anything else by his plays. So after all, a romantic crush which had kept those in my mind proved of great use. No rules govern the nature of biographical writing of course, so one makes up one's own rules, and Arthur Maltby's study of recent lives of Shakespeare (Edwin Mellen Press, 2009) includes interviews which suggest a remarkable liveliness of approach and thought in this field.

Park Honan (1928-2014) took his PhD at the University of London while writing plays for student groups. His London thesis appears as *Browning Characters: A Study in Poetic Technique* (Yale University Press, 1961; Archon, 1969). After adding chapters to William Irvine's *The Book, The Ring, and The Poet* (Bodley Head and McGraw-Hill, 1974) he took a major interest in the art of literary biography. He wrote the first detailed life of Arnold, *Matthew Arnold: A Life* (Weidenfeld, 1981; Harvard University Press, 1983) and then *Jane Austen: Her Life* (Weidenfeld, 1987; 2nd edn. Orion, 1987; 3rd edn. Little Books, 2007). These were preludes to two Elizabethan biographies for Oxford University Press, his *Shakespeare: A Life* (1998, 1999) which has also appeared in translations, and *Christopher Marlowe:*

Poet & Spy (2005, 2007). He has written *Authors' Lives: On Literary Biography and the Arts of Language* (St Martin's Press, 1990) which includes a chapter on 'Shakespeare's Life', and contributed to books about Shakespeare or about literary biography. Some of his ideas are discussed in interviews, and also by K.H. Beetz in *Dictionary of Literary Biography*, 111 (1991), 81–91. In the last years of his life he was working on a biography of T.S. Eliot.

Chapter 5
From Biographies to Bardcom

Peter Holland

I suppose my interest in Shakespeare biography must have begun with childhood trips with my parents to Stratford-upon-Avon, primarily for theatre (Paul Robeson as Othello, Charles Laughton as Bottom, Peter O'Toole as Shylock) but also the obligatory tourist experiences, Shakespeare from cradle to grave, from Birthplace to Holy Trinity, via, in 1964, the quatercentenary exhibition. But I am sure that the true intellectual excitement about the topic began when I read Sam Schoenbaum's *Shakespeare's Lives* (Oxford: Clarendon Press, 1970) when a graduate student. I devoured it in two days, all 800+ pages of it, fascinated by its exploration of the ways in which each biographer's Shakespeare became uncannily – and largely unintentionally – so like the biographer's life, from Rowe's view of Shakespeare in retirement as a gentleman to Lytton Strachey's aesthete and beyond. For all the excellence of Schoenbaum's *William Shakespeare: A Documentary Life* (Oxford: Clarendon Press, 1975), not least as a beautiful piece of book-making, with its superb fold-out facsimiles that reawoke the boy in me, always curious about historical artefacts, I could never warm to it, perhaps because of the sheer size of the volume that made it impossible to curl up with, when, years later, I finally bought a copy. Precisely because of its emphasis on the 'documentary' evidence, it always seemed overly solemn, even when Schoenbaum was at his sharpest in his comments on others' errors and delusions.

Notes for this section can be found on page 67.

My own experience of writing a Shakespeare biography was an unusual one. I was invited, thanks to Ian Donaldson, to write the one for the *Oxford Dictionary of National Biography*. I went to Oxford to talk with Colin Matthew, its founding editor, nervous about his expectations. The memorable conversation established two principles: the first was that he was more than happy with my wish to spend more of my allotted space on the afterlife than the life; the second that he was determined that the entry on Shakespeare should be the longest in the *ODNB*. The latter resulted in something that few have ever experienced with a publisher: repeated updates offering me more and more space. Cromwell has arrived – have another 3,000 words. Churchill's just in – have 2,000 more. The final count was something over 37,000 words and more than 20,000 were spent on Shakespeare after his death. I have not dared to look back at what I wrote for many years but others kindly continue to tell me that my biography is sane and measured and sound. With some pardonable pride I managed to squeeze in references to Shakespeare in the naming of cigars and in other advertising:

> There are cigars named Hamlet, Romeo y Julietta, Falstaff and Antonio y Cleopatra. His own image and his characters have been used to sell, for example, Ford cars, Shell petrol, Schweppes soft drinks and Maxwell House coffee or, since 1986, Coca-Cola, Shreddies breakfast cereal, Typhoo tea and Carling Black Label lager.[1]

In some ways mine was the direct inheritor of Schoenbaum's concern with documentary evidence. It appeared in print in 2004, the same year that Stephen Greenblatt published *Will in the World* (New York: W.W.Norton) with its exhilarating willingness (pun on *will* intentional) to fantasize a meeting between Shakespeare and Campion and other alternative realities for which there is no documentary evidence at all. Less defiant of the absence of proof but equally brilliant came the density of the micro-biography in James Shapiro's *1599: A Year in the Life of William Shakespeare* (New York: HarperCollins, 2005).

Unsurprisingly and although I so enjoyed the writing of Greenblatt and Shapiro, I find myself thrilled by the work of the new documentarians, Schoenbaum's successors, a generation of archive rats who have found extraordinary and unsuspected materials. Some of that new stuff and all the more familiar evidence is now available on *Shakespeare Documented*, the indispensable online resource that the Folger Shakespeare Library created to mark the 400th anniversary of

Shakespeare's death, in collaboration with the British Library, the Shakespeare Birthplace Trust and many more.[2] Its annotation, always scholarly, clear and accurate, is my current go-to place for where we are in our understanding of the material traces. Alongside it I now place a fine collection of articles by those who are closest to the archives: *Shakespeare on Record: Researching an Early Modern Life*, edited by Hannah Leah Crummé (London: The Arden Shakespeare, 2019), the outcome of her work curating a 2016 exhibition at the UK's National Archives.

What's next? Or, more specifically, what's next for me? I still regret that the revised edition of *Shakespeare's Lives* that Schoenbaum published in 1991, for all its incorporation of new material, reduced the space in the section called "Deviations" given to the anti-Stratfordians (many of whom kindly offered to help me by reviewing the drafts of my *ODNB* piece and telling me where I had gone wrong) and, as Schoenbaum put it, he 'also – somewhat more reluctantly – made do without Shakespeare as a character in plays and novels'.[3] The regret is not only because of what he had originally covered so well but also because I find myself ever more strongly intrigued by how Shakespeare is being represented, something I first explored in an article in 2005.[4] Take, for instance, the improbable success of Ben Elton's *Upstart Crow*, originally six episodes on BBC in 2016 and then followed by two more series of six and three Christmas specials, not to mention the publication of the scripts for Series 1 and 2. Elton's creation of a language for Shakespeare to speak in this sitcom – or, as it is sometimes called, bardcom – involved the coining of dozens of completely fake but authentic-sounding words and phrases like *arsingmongle* and *Bolingbrokes*, as in this extract from a YouTube piece of David Mitchell as Shakespeare delivering a message to students on the day when A Level results came out:

> Yes, my jokes aren't funny. But do you really think your hilarious memes will still raise a giggle in the 25th century? They're not even funny now, if you ask me. And what sort of arsingmongle is setting these questions? Did you ever read such Bolingbrokes?[5]

Indeed, the scripts (*Upstart Crow: The Scripts* [London: Penguin, 2018]) include a glossary of these coinings (pp.356-7), as well as fake Elizabethan stage directions, such as "Marlowe doth place his boots upon the table most arrogantly" (p. 188), 'Kate be buried in a book' (p. 185) or 'Bottom speaketh in the manner of an aside, which by strict convention none can overhear' (p. 254). Elton adds his own commentary on the scripts in footnotes so that, when Robert Greene, the villain of the series, finally explains why the series is called *Upstart Crow* (series 1, episode 4) by saying 'this upstart crow is ever more advanced in the world, beautifying himself in the feathers of a gentleman', Elton attaches a footnote that 'Here Greene quotes a passage from his own description of Shakespeare in his *Groatsworth of Wit*, a book that would have been completely forgotten had it not contained a short passage slagging off Shakespeare' (p. 90).

The energy, wit and imagination of *Upstart Crow*, all strikingly absent from Elton's commissioned script for Kenneth Branagh's disappointing film of Shakespeare in melancholic retirement, *All Is True* (2019), is worth celebrating but so too is the bardcom's fascination with a domestic Shakespeare, travelling regularly back to Stratford-upon-Avon, delayed by the transport system, and ending each episode, in a rather moving expression of domestic companionship, sat with his wife side by side by the fire, both smoking pipes, and chatting about what has been happening. After a story-line involving a Stratford farmer called Duncan MacBuff in which at one point Shakespeare has a vision of a milk jug ('Is this a milk jug which I see before me?...The handle toward my hand? Come, let me clutch thee', p. 126), Anne suggests to Will: 'You know, husband, all these doings'd make a really good play':

> *Will.* Yes, you're right. Of course! A light and breezy comedy about a laughable misunderstanding over some milk.
>
> *Anne.* Well, actually, I was thinking more of the weird sisters, the ghost at the feast, the conscience-stricken wife endlessly washing her hands in the night. You know, a proper blood-and-guts thriller.
>
> *Will.* No, no, I think comedy's the way to go. 'Two Milky Jugs' by William Shakespeare. (p. 148)

To which Elton adds a footnote: 'If Shakespeare did write this play it is lost in the mists of time. Which is a great shame.' (p.148).

Elton's vision of Shakespeare as sitcom dad is no less scholarly than Greenblatt's imagined meetings – as has often been pointed out, Elton's uncle was Sir Geoffrey Elton, the most brilliant Tudor historian of his generation. There is also an intriguing convergence between the tv sitcom and its subject as Elton has turned the series into a play. As the advance publicity announces,

> David Mitchell makes his West End debut in Ben Elton's stage adaptation of the critically acclaimed BBC tv sitcom, *Upstart Crow*. This

all-new comedy – written especially for the stage – will see Mitchell once more don the bald wig and bardish coddling pouch in his iconic characterization of Will Shakespeare.[6]

More or less sold out as I write this, still three months before the show opens, this too is biography, one more of Shakespeare's lives, another exploration of the genre of plays about the playwright, like, say, George Bernard Shaw's puppet-play *Shakes vs Shav* (1949), his last completed play. In its intervention into the cultural meaning that the concept of the originating author has become it speaks eloquently of what we wish Shakespeare to have been, while knowing this both is and is not him.

Peter Holland is McMeel Family Professor in Shakespeare Studies at the University of Notre Dame. Prior to that he was Director of the Shakespeare Institute, Stratford-upon-Avon. He was Editor of *Shakespeare Survey* for 19 years and is co-General Editor for *Oxford Shakespeare Topics, Arden Shakespeare in the Theatre* and the *Arden Shakespeare 4th Series*. He has edited many Shakespeare plays including *A Midsummer Night's Dream* (Oxford) and *Coriolanus* (Arden 3rd series). He is the author of over 150 articles and book chapters on Shakespeare, Garrick, pantomime and other topics. Current projects include a monograph on *Shakespeare and Forgetting* and editing *King Lear* for *Arden 4*.

Notes

1. 'William Shakespeare' in *Oxford Dictionary of National Biography*, online edition, accessed 30 November 2019.
2. See https://shakespearedocumented.folger.edu/, accessed 30 November 2019.
3. S.Schoenbaum, *Shakespeare's Lives*, revised edition (Oxford: Oxford University Press, 1991), x.
4. 'Dramatizing the Dramatist,' *Shakespeare Survey 58* (Cambridge University Press, 2005), 137-47.
5. 'Shakespeare's A-Level Results Day Message', 2018, A Dose of David Mitchell on *YouTube*, accessed 26 August 2019, <https://www.youtube.com/watch?v=eTVYNEFQs-0>, my transcription.
6. https://upstartcrowthecomedy.com/, accessed 30 November 2019.

Chapter 6
Shakespeare Biography and Identity Politics

Lois Potter

After Kate Winslett had played Iris Murdoch in the film *Iris,* she told an interviewer how much she admired the writer and was naturally asked which of the novels she liked best. She replied that she had only "dipped into" a few, but she admired Murdoch enormously as a person. What she really meant, as far as I could tell, was that she admired her character's strong personality and extensive love life.

Well, all the world loves a love story. Virgil's myriad readers were more interested in Aeneas' desertion of Dido than in his founding of Rome. The speaker of Lyly's prologue to *Campaspe* (1582) admits that 'we, calling Alexander from his grave, seek only who was his love'. Shakespeare himself, at least at the beginning of his career, was known mainly as a love poet. The author of *The Return from Parnassus*, a university play in which contemporary writers are discussed, referred to him as the author of the two poems about 'Adon's love and Lucrece' rape' and went on to wish that he would write about something more serious than 'love's foolish lazy languishment'. He did not go on to suggest that Shakespeare himself must have been a great lover; that was left for whoever told John Manningham the story about Shakespeare beating Burbage to the rendezvous with a stage-struck lady.

The story is too good to be true, yet every biographer is happy to include it. It's an example of why biographies of writers are often more popular than the works of the writers. Like Park Honan, I agree that there are no rules for writing a biography, and I have always had to see what I'd written before I could deduce the principles on which I must have written it. In my essay for Richard Bradford's collection, *Literary Biography*, I have already talked about the problem of being, almost certainly, the biographer who had the least in common with Shakespeare. This problem was no doubt exacerbated by my unwillingness to try to see Shakespeare as having anything in common with me – though of course I had to recognize that *The Life of William Shakespeare* had ended up being the story of a competent professional like me rather than the exciting rebel that so many biographers hope to find (and, I think, would like to be).

My book was called a 'critical biography', and it took me some time to see what this meant. What I would say, now, is that I was writing about Shakespeare's works as products of a conscious literary and theatrical craftsman rather than as extended speeches made by a character (Shakespeare) in a play (his life). This latter experience is what I think many readers want. It happened to Frank Harris after he had been reading Shakespeare again and again: 'out of the myriad voices in the plays, I began to hear more and more insistent the accents of one voice' (*The Man Shakespeare and His Tragic Life Story*, ix). Other biographers have also been convinced that they could hear the 'real' voice of the author in any speech that coincided with what we already know about Shakespeare's life. To me, Orsino's 'Let still the woman take/ An elder than herself' is dramatically and comically right, since, though he doesn't know it, the male speaker is pontificating to a woman who is longing to do precisely what he is telling her to do, and I think that this, in performance, would be most likely to strike an audience. But for many biographers, of whom Stephen Greenblatt is the best known, the interest of this statement lies in the sound of Shakespeare's voice behind it: 'How could he have written Orsino's words without in some sense bringing his own life, his disappointment, frustration, and loneliness, to bear upon them?' (*Will in the World*, 124).

Anything is possible 'in some sense', so one can assume that Shakespeare's private life, including many things about which we know nothing, is somehow infused into his work and that some of this, at least, would have been clear to him. But all that I can imagine him wanting an audience to recognize are the metatheatrical references that always give pleasure, like – also in *Twelfth Night* – 'If this were played upon a stage now, I could condemn it as an improbable fiction'. A lot of the audience, if they were regular theatre-goers, might have enjoyed the reminder, in *Hamlet*, that the actors of Hamlet and Polonius had formerly played Brutus and Julius Caesar – something that, of course, is lost on a modern audience. Maybe the jokes about dramatic characters named Will or William (if they *were* intended, which I rather doubt) would have resonated with whatever fraction of the audience happened to know the author's name. But what I really want to know is how Shakespeare felt about his profession, both the acting and the writing. Did he agree with Samuel Johnson that 'Punch has no feelings'? Yet, even as I ask this question, I worry that I have started playing identity politics – trying to get credit for being a particularly sensitive person, or having the 'right' kind of views, rather than for having offered anything particularly new or relevant about Shakespeare.

In *That Shakespeherian Rag* (1986), Terry Hawkes dug into the biographies of well-known Shakespeare scholars and showed that they often had reactionary political and social views. Since then, there has been something of a demand for full disclosure on the part of everyone who writes (no more 'it is generally thought'; we want 'I think'). Novelists are pressured into having blogs so that their readers can feel a special relationship with them, and now even academics are urged to let themselves become public figures. Biography, like everything else, is subject to the pendulum swing that, for me, is the only obvious principle of critical history. When it is fashionable to be super-rational and tough-minded, as in the mid-twentieth century, critics ridicule the sentimentality, not only of Shakespeare's characters, but of critical responses to them. When the pendulum swings in the other direction, critics point out the insensitivity of characters – and their critical predecessors — to the feelings of others, especially those who have traditionally been disadvantaged or marginalized. No play of Shakespeare's is free of views that belong to another age. But even to point out that their general attitude is one of respect for authority figures, and ridicule of eccentricity or 'difference' in all forms, is to risk accusations of elitism, conservatism, and even racism.

If it sometimes seems as if we are losing our sense of humour, it is because the movement from intentionalist criticism to presentist and reader response criticism now has its parallel in the public sphere. What matters is not what you meant, or thought you meant, but what someone else felt when they heard or read it. Almost everyone who spends any time in the public eye soon discovers that it is better never to make any jokes at all. Shakespeare discovered this in the official reaction to the character formerly known as Oldcastle. And, once the biographer enters the public sphere, the internet trolls move in, convinced that anyone who is given so much attention deserves to be punished for it. Their attitude was beautifully expressed by Marlowe in lines that I've been longing to quote for years. They are spoken by one of the killers during the St Bartholomew's Massacre:

> I am disguised and none knows who I am,
> And therefore mean to murder all I meet.

Maybe, as has recently been suggested with regard to political life, this new development will mean that only a certain type of person will want to be a writer. The main beneficiary is the reader who doesn't have time to read all the famous literary works, or the biographies of their authors, or the criticisms of the biographies. How delightful to find that the secret views of all these people are so morally reprehensible that reading them would be a positive crime!

Lois Potter, Ned B. Allen Professor Emerita of the University of Delaware, has published on Milton, English Civil War literature, the theatrical history of *Twelfth Night* and *Othello*, and Robin Hood. She edited *The Two Noble Kinsmen* for the Arden Shakespeare and Pericles for the Norton Complete Works (2016). Her most recent book is *The Life of William Shakespeare* (Wiley-Blackwell 2012).

Chapter 7
Shakespeare and Biography

René Weis

When my biography of Shakespeare was contracted, by John Murray in London and Henry Holt in New York, it was on the understanding that its audience would be the general reader. I had written trade books for Hamish Hamilton, Vintage, Penguin, and Knopf, and was expected to produce a Shakespeare biography that would be an 'open' book. What intrigued the publishers about my proposal was its two-pronged approach: a use of specific contemporary contexts for Shakespeare's Stratford and London and an in-depth mining of the plays and poems for clues about the life and mind of Shakespeare. The former would entail a detailed, house-by-house, reconstruction of the topography of 1590s Stratford-upon-Avon and draw on an intimate insider's view of Elizabethan England, in particular through the Jesuit John Gerard's brilliantly evocative autobiography. Gerard was born the same year as Shakespeare and Marlowe. His extensive account of his mission, a life on the run, of secret hiding places, capture, and flight from the Tower, may be the most authentic eyewitness account to survive from the age of Shakespeare. No-one else captures so intimately the feverish atmosphere of London and the Catholic English Midlands, as seen from the underground, as this hugely charismatic priest who moved fearlessly through the sectarian hinterland of the country's religious fault line.

One of the most damaging clichés about Shakespeare and life-writing, repeated at times even by scholars, is that known hard facts about Shakespeare fit on the back of an envelope. Few statements could be further from the truth, though it is the case that the 'hard' documents attaching to Shakespeare's name do not necessarily tell us what we would most want to know.

Take for example Shakespeare's last will and testament. It is a long and detailed account of the belongings and bequests of the respected landowner of New Place, Stratford-upon-Avon. It is of huge intrinsic interest, of course, as social history and is revealing, albeit at most tangentially, about his relationship with his daughters Susanna and Judith. Thus the late change to the will regarding Judith almost certainly reflects the dying Shakespeare's response to the local scandal that had engulfed her husband-to-be shortly after the first drafting of the will. As for the 'second-best bed' and its alleged bearing on the poet's supposed estrangement from his wife Anne, this is now largely considered to be a fantasy of biographers in search of stories to complement narratives about Shakespeare's putative affair with a 'dark' mistress in London.

If we did not have Shakespeare's last will, we would want to invent it; but *not* the version that has survived. It tells us nothing about what the greatest writer of all time may have thought about writing, what he made of his own huge achievements, what he felt when his little boy died in the summer of 1596, what he thought of being a father of boy-girl twins, whether he was closer to his father than to his mother, where he stood on the big issue of the day, the long-range fall-out from the Reformation that twice in his life-time, under two different monarchs, threatened to engulf his country in civil strife: from 1586 to 1588, when he was in his twenties (Elizabeth I: the Babington conspiracy, Mary Queen of Scots and the Armada), and again in November 1605 (King James: the Powder Plot), when he had recently written *Othello*. If though Shakespeare could talk to us now, he might reply to all these questions by referring, respectively with regard to these questions, to the *Tempest* (the poet as creator-magician), *Romeo and Juliet* and *King John* (dead children, a mother grieving for her son), *The Comedy of Errors* and *Twelfth Night* (twins and cross-gender twins), *Hamlet* (fathers and sons), *Coriolanus* (mother and son), and to his English histories as an imaginative wrestling with the sectarian politics of his time; not to mention *King Lear* and *Macbeth* (1605-6), both of them Powder Plot plays.

Shakespeare did not keep a diary, unlike Ben Jonson whose commonplace book *Timber or Discoveries* contains an off-the-cuff tribute to Shakespeare that perfectly chimes with his famous elegy on his dead friend in the 1623 Folio. The more the pity, perhaps, but Shakespeare's works, two long poems, a cycle of sonnets, and some forty plays cannot possibly be ignored in writing about his life: they were after all a major part of that life and the very reason why we are interested in him to this day.

Why then, I wondered, were biographers quite so squeamish about using the works? After all they demonstrably refer to the times he lived in and even, on one famous occasion, refer explicitly to one of his friends.

Naturally an approach proposing to draw on literature for biographical nuggets would require considerable tact. It would be self-evidently injudicious to read Shakespeare's plays as if they were Wordsworth's *Prelude* or Proust's *A la recherche du temps perdu*, works explicitly reconfiguring lived lives into literature, with the subjective 'I' of the author artfully recast to stand for humankind's wider experience. At the same time to treat the works as if they existed in a rarified imaginative zone, cut loose from lived experience, seemed counter-intuitive. Shakespeare lived in a historical context that we know very well. He was not after all Homer where all we have by way of evidence and context are the two epic poems. With regard to Homer, the most we can do by way of 'biography' is to profile the poet from internal evidence: as someone who knows the world of the Bronze Age Aegean intimately, who knows the topography of Greece and Asia Minor, of the Trojan plain and of Ithaca, who values above all else loyalty, faith, hospitality. But all that would be inferential and entirely speculative.

The case of Shakespeare is altogether different. Probably no passage in the works illustrates a demonstrable convergence of his own life and fiction as strikingly as Imogen's reply to Lucius in *Cymbeline*. When asked her master's name, she replies 'Richard du Champ. If I do lie and do / No harm by it, though the gods hear, I hope / They'll pardon it'. Richard du Champ is Richard Field ('du Champ' – 'of the Field') from Bridge Street in Stratford-upon-Avon. He was three years older than Shakespeare and the two boys would have attended the same grammar school in the town. Over thirty years later Field printed Shakespeare's long poems *Venus and Adonis* and *The Rape of Lucrece*. By then he had married the French widow of a Huguenot printer to whom he had been apprenticed. In case the allusion to Field needs firming up, Imogen's female page name is 'Fidele' ('loyal and faithful'), almost an anagram of Field. It is not impossible that the reference to Field by a character styled 'Faithful' might be a gesture of gratitude and friendship by the middle-aged Shakespeare, by now probably back in his grand *domus* in Stratford-upon-Avon. We will never know why Field is singled out for special mention in *Cymbeline*, but the fact that he is so provides proof of Shakespeare's relaxed sense of the fluid boundaries between fact and fiction, of the local here-and-now habitations of his plays; as much in *Cymbeline* as in the Induction to the much earlier play *The Taming of the Shrew*, which seems set in his mother's home village of Wilmcote near Stratford.

While some of the plays and poems allude openly to contemporary events, politics, and people (for example *Henry V*, *Hamlet*, *Macbeth*, *Coriolanus*, *Cymbeline*), others may do so more obliquely and more intimately as already suggested, notably *King John*, *Romeo and Juliet*, *Twelfth Night*, and *Pericles*, a play which, it is argued persuasively by its Arden 3 editor, may well allude to the birth of Shakespeare's granddaughter Elizabeth. The prominence in that play, commonly dated to 1608, of the (almost) miracle-working physician Cerimon, may well point to Dr John Hall who had married Susanna Shakespeare the previous year. Their daughter Elizabeth was baptised in February 1608. Under these circumstances it is not unreasonable to see allusions to the Shakespeare family, to Susanna, Dr Hall, and Elizabeth in Thaisa, Cerimon, and Marina. It may not tell us much, if anything, about the play as literature, but it does indicate, as with Richard Field, that Shakespeare did not feel inhibited about writing from his own private experience of life in his plays. That in itself may take us closer to who he was: perhaps more of a subjective, proto-Romantic writer than was previously thought? In a wonderful passage in a letter to his brothers, a young English poet, himself perhaps Shakespeare's most instinctively perceptive critic, remarked that 'A man's life of any worth is a continual allegory – and very few eyes can see the mystery of his life ... Lord Byron cuts a figure – but he is not figurative – Shakespeare led a life of allegory; his works are the comments on it.' (John Keats).

A major challenge facing any biographer of Shakespeare is the long shadow cast by Samuel Schoenbaum's *William Shakespeare: A Documentary Life* (1975). Schoenbaum's masterly book is not in fact a biography but a biographically-led anaylsis of extant documents relating to Shakespeare, shrewdly fleshed out with a history of the London theatres and Shakespeare's involvement with the Lord

Chamberlain's and King's Men. Schoenbaum's determination to turn biography into a scientific enterprise resulted in a form of rigorous, at times almost doctrinaire, positivism that excluded anything from biographical enquiry that had not survived as hard copy in the records. His book at times reads like a commentary on E. K. Chambers's two-volume *William Shakespeare: A Study of Facts and Problems* (1930), to which it is significantly indebted.

In my own Stratford-centric biography I disagreed with Schoenbaum in particular on what he considered to be the anecdotal traditions deriving from seventeenth-century Stratford and Warwickshire. Thus he discarded the most important early testimony about Shakespeare, Nicholas Rowe's 1709 biography. Schoenbaum downplayed the trustworthiness of Rowe's account because he could not corroborate, let alone triangulate, some of Rowe's more outlandish-sounding assertions about the dramatist, notably Shakespeare's alleged poaching and his sudden exile from Stratford.

But at least some of Rowe's claims *are* backed up significantly, as even Schoenbaum had to admit, by other early accounts to the same effect. Rowe's acknowledged source was Betterton, whose 'veneration for the memory of Shakespeare having engaged him to make a journey into Warwickshire, on purpose to gather up what remains he could of a name for which he had so great a value'. (Rowe) It is in Rowe that we first read that Shakespeare's wife was called Hathaway. It was not until 1836, when the Stratford antiquarian Robert B. Wheler discovered the Shakespeare marriage bond of 28 November 1582, that the accuracy of Rowe's identification was confirmed. I believe that Rowe may similarly be right about Shakespeare's poaching at Charlecote. Why after all would a glover's son from a Midlands market town suddenly turn up on the London theatre scene, unless he was 'encouraged' to leave his home town by powerful people, like the Lucys of Charlecote. When Betterton visited Stratford Shakespeare's daughter and certainly his granddaughter may still have been alive. So would have been members of his sister Joan's family in Henley Street and friends of the Shakespeares. It is another local rumour, first reported in the eighteenth century by John Jordan, a Stratford antiquarian (whom Schoenbaum also distrusts), that helped to pinpoint Shakespeare's mother's house in Wilmcote. Jordan did not quite get it right, but we now know that he was out by one house (more accurately 'farm') only. There was no reason for anyone in Stratford to invent things about Shakespeare; certainly not before the Garrick Jubilee of 1769 after which the age of bardolatry launched Shakespeare as a tourist brand. By neglecting Stratford-upon-Avon biographers almost wilfully cut themselves off from the local post-1616 afterlife of the poet. We would do well to remember that key documents such as the bond and the poet's testament were found centuries later in his home town.

René Weis is a Professor of English at University College London. His publications include *Shakespeare Revealed: a Biography* (John Murray, London, 2007; variant longer version pub. in New York as *Shakespeare Unbound*, Henry Holt & Co, 2007). He has edited *Romeo and Juliet* for the Arden Shakespeare Third Series, *Henry IV*, Part 2 for Oxford, and selected plays of John Webster (incl. *The Duchess of Malfi* and *The White Devil*) for Oxford. His biography of Marie Duplessis, *The Real Traviata*, appeared from Oxford in 2015. His book *The Yellow Cross* (Viking & Penguin, 2000) has been published in seven languages.

Chapter 8
Shakeshafte

Rowan Williams

Preface

In August 1581, Alexander Hoghton, of Lea and Hoghton Tower in Lancashire, died, after making a will in which he left bequests to a number of members of his household – a large one, as befitted one of the wealthiest men in the region, occupying an ample and spectacularly situated mansion not far from Preston. Among the beneficiaries are Fulk Gillom (who can be traced with some likelihood as belonging to a Chester family connected with the productions of the guild plays in the city) and William Shakeshafte. In addition to receiving legacies, these two are also recommended to a neighbour, Sir Thomas Hesketh, for patronage and/or employment; the context clearly suggests that they are involved with providing entertainments for the household.

Nothing more can be learned for sure about Shakeshafte. But since Hoghton's will was first published in the nineteenth century, the similarity of the name to that of a better-known sixteenth-century figure has generated a wealth of speculation. A local tradition was unearthed that Shakespeare had worked with a Catholic family in Lancashire, and John Aubrey's report that Shakespeare had in his youth been 'a schoolmaster in the country' was prayed in aid. The possible Catholic connections and sympathies of Shakespeare at various points of his life gave the thesis added plausibility for some; and Lord Strange, later Earl of Derby and an early patron of Shakespeare, had close links with Lancashire and its gentry families. More significantly, it emerged that John Cottam, schoolmaster in Stratford from 1579 to 1582, came from a family living near Hoghton Tower.

Cottam and the Hoghtons were loyal to the 'old religion'; and when the Jesuit, Edmund Campion, toured the north of England in 1580–1, he stayed with different members of the Hoghton family, among other Catholic gentry households. Converted to Catholicism after a brilliant Oxford career, Campion had moved abroad to study for the priesthood, joined the Jesuits and made a stellar reputation in Europe, spending time at the court of the Holy Roman emperor Rudolf II in Prague. He returned to England in 1580 – along with Thomas Cottam, brother of the Stratford schoolmaster, also a Jesuit priest.

At this period, Catholic missioners from abroad were regarded by Elizabeth I's government as automatically treasonous, given that the Pope in 1569 had sanctioned the removal by force or assassination of the Queen. Their reputation was much the same as that of Al Qaeda in the present context, though very few indeed actually supported violence or rebellion. Both Cottam and Campion were executed in 1581 by the usual barbaric method of partial hanging followed by disembowelling. Campion was made a saint by the Roman Catholic Church in 1970.

So there is a strong likelihood that Campion was either at Hoghton Tower or at Alexander Hoghton's other residence at Lea during some period in 1580–1. Whoever William Shakeshafte really was must have been there at the same time. Scholars differ very sharply about the likelihood of the identification of Shakeshafte with the young man from Stratford; several leading Shakespearean experts such as Katherine Duncan-Jones and Jonathan Bate believe that the Lancashire connection is wholly discredited; but others still consider it a possibility, given the slender but strong chain of connections with what can be securely known of Shakespeare.

Short of decisive new documentary evidence, it is unlikely that the question will ever be settled. But that at least allows for a 'fantasia' (borrowing Thornton Wilder's term for his historical novel, The Ides of March*) on the events of these years – particularly on what a Campion and a Shakespeare might have had to say to each other: the intelligence of the martyr and the intelligence of the poet. And that is what this play attempts.*

Practically all the names are taken from Hoghton's will or other documents from the same period and area. Hoghton's exiled older brother was actually called Thomas, like the younger half-brother who inherited his estate; since this half-brother appears here, I have renamed the older brother William to avoid confusion. Similarly, I have rechristened Roger, Margaret Crichlow's husband, as Walter to distinguish him from Roger Livesey. There is a codicil to Hoghton's will revoking, without explanation, the legacy to Margaret. 'Hastings' was one of several assumed names used by Campion in his travels.

It is worth remembering that this is a period in which accent has nothing to do with class. Gentry and servants sound much the same, and they will all sound rather different from a southerner like Will or an internationally mobile intellectual like Hastings/Campion.

*

Characters

The Family
ALEXANDER HOGHTON, of Hoghton Tower
THOMAS HOGHTON, his younger brother
MARGARET (MEG) CRICHLOW, his daughter

*

The Household
ROGER LIVESEY, steward of Hoghton Tower
ROB TOMLINSON
MARGERY GERRARD
FULK GILLOM
WILL SHAKESHAFTE
THOMASIN
ALICE
SUSANNA

*

EDWARD HASTINGS/ EDMUND CAMPION

*

The setting is Hoghton Tower, Lancashire: for these purposes, a general 'Great Hall' space, door towards back, with hearth downstage right, settle, long table (downstage left), benches, a couple of stools; and a staircase to an upper level. The action takes place between the winter of 1580 and the summer of 1581.

Scene I

[*Heavy knocks on a door.* THOMAS HOGHTON – *brisk, late fifties – enters noisily, discarding riding cloak, etc., to servants*]

THOMAS [*loudly*] Alex! Alex! Roger! Alex! Roger, where are you?
[ROGER LIVESEY – *in his forties; undemonstrative but capable of some very strong emotions – enters in nightgown, dishevelled and irritable*]
ROGER For Christ's sake, Master Tom! D'you know what hour it is?
THOMAS I'm not here for my health. Where's Alex?
ROGER I don't care what you do or don't do for your health, but you might think about your brother's.
THOMAS [*slightly chastened*] I know, I know. How does he go on?
ROGER Not good. Six nights out of seven he won't be asleep till around now.
THOMAS [*pause*] How long?
ROGER Doctor says nine months, maybe twelve, no more.
[ALEXANDER HOGHTON – *early sixties, heavy and formidable, slowed down by physical pain – has appeared at the head of the stairs, in nightgown*]
ALEX Nine if I'm lucky, twelve if I'm not. What the hell is all this, Tom?
ROGER Master Tom can come up to your chamber; you need to be back in bed.
ALEX Well I'm awake. What's the use? [*comes slowly and painfully downstairs*] Roger, get me a... [*looks around; Roger pulls up a stool to the table*] Ay, that'll do. Now, find yourself some work; the whole bloody house'll be awake thanks to Tom here. [*Roger goes*] This had better be important or I'll have your guts.
THOMAS [*pauses*] Have you slept?
ALEX Not above an hour. Now: if I've got nine months left, I don't fancy wasting them waiting for you to tell me what you've got for me. Bad news, right?
THOMAS It's Tom Cottam.
ALEX They've taken him?
THOMAS Last week in Dover, soon as he'd landed. I guess he'll be put to the question any day.

ALEX Christ. How do you know?

THOMAS Letter from Jack in the midlands. He sent it to one of our people in Preston and they brought it to me last night. I rode straight here.

ALEX You'll want something. Roger! [*Turns back to Thomas*] What's Jack Cottam after apart from prayers? because by God he'll need those almost as much as Tom will. [*Roger comes in*] Get us some ale.

ROGER Trouble?

ALEX Bad trouble. Tom Cottam, Tarnacre.

ROGER Ay. Taken, is he?

ALEX Taken. It's his brother writing to us, the schoolmaster down in Warwickshire, remember? [*To Thomas*] So what does he want? [*To Roger*] Ale.

THOMAS Perhaps Roger should stay a moment. It's about the household [*sits*].

ALEX How do you mean?

THOMAS Tom Cottam came back to England with some of the Company, and he sent one or two of them to the Midlands with his list of known men. Jack Cottam introduced a few of his lads from the school to them. They'll have their names any minute if they haven't got them already. Jack says he'll stay there as long as he can, but he thinks the lads need to get out before someone starts taking an interest. Specially as he thinks one or two might be headed overseas. He needs an answer soon as we can.

ALEX So he wants us to take them here? Bloody maniac. Doesn't he know they're watching us already? [*turns towards fire*] After all the fuss about William, God rest his stupid soul? Roger remembers that all right, don't you Roger? [*To Tom*] Sanctimonious old bastard never forgave you or me. We had enough trouble then to last a lifetime, with the agents round yours and round here, sniffing for priests in the barns and the shithouse... [*Back to others; more loudly*] And so: we take on a few young men with Midlands voices and suspicious backgrounds trying to find passage on a ship? God help us; Jack's as big a fool as William was. We might as well write to the justices and say, here's a nest of foreign papists, come and collect them and while you're at it we'll be glad to oblige you on the rack and kindly pull out our fingernails.

THOMAS Ay, well; Can't quarrel with that. But what he says is there's just one he wants us to take that he thinks might pass up here. Sixteen or so. Plays and sings, writes a good hand, he says, not just one of the yokels. His father's an alderman or some such.

ALEX One of ours?

THOMAS Well, Jack's got a bit to say about that. Sounds like the old man's playing both sides. He's paid the fines, but he paid for pulling down the images and whitewashing the church too. Jack says he's a close old bastard and pays the fines for not going to church so that no-one has a chance to arrest him for his debts when he's out and about; says it's cheaper that way.

ALEX [*laughs shortly*] Sounds like a proper hero of the faith. Is his son the same, then?

THOMAS Jack says he's been listening to the priests when they come and he doesn't know what he should do, and he's not happy about his father's ways.

ALEX Let's see this letter, then [*Thomas passes it over, Alexander scans it, Thomas wanders over to the hearth*]. Well I see what he means about him passing up here; the name's nearly right. There's Shakeshaftes ten miles away. Maybe they've got a long-lost cousin down south that they're just about to discover. Roger, what do you reckon? Can we find room for a – what, for God' sake? Player, tutor, dogsbody? Along with that other lad from Chester who's coming?

ROGER I suppose. But you're not telling me you want him here, are you? Him and his little trail of agents running after? It's no time for you to be giving yourself more to trouble you.

THOMAS If we get straight back to Jack, today, we may be ahead of any agents. And by the time they've picked it up, he should be here and we can sort out the story. [*ALEX gets up, begins walking back to the stairs*] But you'd better finish the letter.

ALEX God, you mean there's more? What?

THOMAS It's one of Tom Cottam's friends from the Company. He's travelling up here. He'll need a place to come and go from a bit.

ALEX Like I said; it's not as if Hoghtons escaped notice round here. Here we are, lads, come and arrest us, eh? [*sits again*] Come and pick up the servants and the family and find out what the old man's being saying in his cups, and... [*trails away, rubbing forehead, very tired*]

ROGER [*Fiercely*] You've earned some peace; what business is it of yours if some fancy priest from overseas wants to come and stir things up? We can wait for changes. We don't need...

ALEX Shut up, Roger. [*Silence. Reads. Sighs*] Thing is, I'll be dead in the year if they're right. There's not a lot they can do to scare me. And I'm going to have to face my Maker and say to him, I couldn't be bothered when it would cost me nothing or next to nothing. I don't fancy that. I've got enough on my slate to need a few good works in the balance.

THOMAS [*pause; then*] Shall I get a message to Jack?

ALEX All right. Yes. Get him a message, today. We'll take his young man. And I guess we've no choice but to take this priest from the Company and all. Roger, you're sitting there like a wet Sunday. [*ROGER opens his mouth to snap back, thinks better of it, shakes head/tuts*] Get some bloody *ale* for Christ's sake! And another gown. I'm cold. [*Rises slowly and starts for the stairs*]

[*Blackout*]

Scene II

[*MARGARET CRICHLOW – mid-twenties, can seem older, self-possessed, chilly –comes in, rapidly, followed by ROGER with ROB TOMLINSON, local tenant farmer, about Roger's age, awkwardly in the background*]

MARGARET You're telling me he won't see me?

ROGER I am. I'll not have him worried at like a fox with the dogs.

MARGARET I *need to see him,* Roger. He owes me that, for Christ's sake. Walter has to know about the money.

ROGER Walter can bloody wait. You know how sick your father is, he's not slept again, he's got guests coming, I've got business with Rob here to settle before noon, there's two new servant lads to see and I'm damned if I'm letting you upset the whole bloody household. Again.

MARGARET [*Level and arctic*] I'm not forgetting this, Roger. And I'm not just going away.

ROGER Right now that's just what you're doing, mistress. There's no-one here with time for you.

MARGARET Never is, is there? Never has been. But there will be soon. Think on.

[*She walks out: fast, bristling*]

ROGER Oh Christ Almighty. [*Sits heavily on the edge of the table; Rob walks closer*] He'll have to see her some day. Force of bloody nature, that woman. [*Gathers himself, turns fully to Rob*] Anyroad, business. It's two weeks. He comes in two weeks' time. Edward Hastings.

ROB Is that his name?

ROGER It's his name while he's here. You know how it is.

ROB So is he one of this – Company, then?

ROGER That's what Master Alex says. I think they've told him who it really is, 'cause he's jumpy about it. My guess is he's a big fish and there's a small army of government fishermen after him. [*dry*] Great news for the rest of us.

ROB [*flops down on bench*] Can't get used to this, Roger. You get these priests coming from France, Low Countries, wherever, dressed up like players, feathers in their hats and garters round their bloody knees, calling theirselves by all kinds of fancy names and laughing to theirselves. Like bloody players. And they tell us that if we go to the Sacrament down in the parish, we're – what did that last bugger say? – eating at the table of demons. [*Gets up, downstage*] Christ almighty; poor old Sir Philip in the parish, he's a clothheaded old sod as spends more time in the alehouse than the church, but he's no demon. Tell you what, Roger, you know I'm all for the old religion, else I wouldn't be here, God help me, but I can't think these hard young men in fancy hats with fancy language are what we need. All right; Elizabeth Tudor's a heretic perhaps, same as Sir Philip, and the service in English sounds bloody daft to me, but God looks after his own and likely when the Queen weds or comes to her senses, we'll –

ROGER [*interrupts*] Look, I've said it all to Alex, Rob, more times than I've had hot dinners. But I don't know who's in the right. Fancy young gents from overseas, from the Company or the, what d'you call it, seminary, you can say what you like but they're not fools or cowards. It's not the hats and the stockings they think about when the hangman's cutting their balls off and sizing them up for quartering.

ROB All very well, Rodge. All very well for them, if they want to risk having their balls off and their bowels out, good luck to them and no, they're no cowards. [*Sits again, looks at hearth*] But it's us too. When the agents come, it's us they look at and it's our balls and bowels they may be sizing up and all. Like I said – like players: only, *they* know the play; they've read the story, and we've not.

ROGER Ay well. [*Slips off table*] Talking of players, the new lads arrived yesterday and I need to see them. Margery's bringing them over. Fulk Gillom up from Chester, and this young lad from down south, from Jack Cottam's school.

ROB You said he was –

ROGER Ay, he's got a name while he's here too, Will Shakeshafte. Should be easy to remember.

ROB Is he some kin to Francis Shakeshafte over to Warrington?

ROGER If it helps to think so.

ROB Like that, then?

ROGER Like that. You watch what you say about him or Hastings. Specially in the Charnock direction.

ROB Do you reckon the Crichlows...

ROGER Better safe – here they come, anyroad. Bugger off, Rob. And remember when Hastings comes – he's not likely to be anyone's fool, so don't play the fool with him. I'll collect you when I've done with these two. It's Ashcrofts this morning.

ROB [*grunts, gets up and moves away to exit, as MARGERY GERRARD – twentyish, handsome, a friendly but sharp manner – comes in with FULK and WILL; late teens, both of them, Fulk a bit earnest and slow, Will physically slight and restless*].

MARGERY Morning Mr Roger; morning Rob. These are the new lads just come. This one's Fulk, this one's Will. [*Grins*] Will's the foreigner.

ROGER Left you alone so far, have they? [*To Fulk and Will*] Well let's have a look at you. Off you go, love [*Margery exits, Roger sits on bench*]. You know where you've come to?

FULK Me dad used to come here years back. He was the man who made the dresses for the players in Chester for the summer plays. He used to bring the stuff up here in winter sometimes,

when they were playing at the Hall for Christmas. I come when I was ten, me and me little brother, and I...
ROGER All right, all right, I don't want all your touching memories. You can sit if you want. [*They sit at the table*] So you know about the Hoghtons?
FULK Some, sir.
WILL Nothing much, sir. Except what Master Cottam says.
ROGER And what does he say?
WILL That Hoghtons have one of the great houses in Lancashire, that they hold to the old religion –
ROGER Like you do.
WILL [*pauses*] Like – I do.
ROGER Come on, lad, you need to do better than that if you're to manage here. I know you're here because Jack Cottam thinks there's danger for his young men who've been talking with the priests from overseas, but this isn't a safe place like Flanders or the bloody emperor's court. If you're here, you take the same risks. You need to know it's worth it.
WILL [*expressionless*] Yes sir.
ROGER I know it wasn't your choice to come.
WILL [*the same*] No sir.
ROGER Well... Anyroad, there's more you need to know [*across to sit on table as before*]. Master Alex is a sick man. It comes and goes, but the doctor knows there's a tumour and it'll likely kill him. So you keep out of his way and you don't make trouble in the village. Anything here that draws attention is trouble, right? The agents will be around and they'll be glad to pay us a visit and maybe more. Fulk, you know about the master's brother, that built the Hall?
FULK The one who went abroad and...
ROGER Ay, he went abroad so as not to pay the church-fines, and they confiscated his land, and Master Alex and his other brother, they worked to keep him out so that he wouldn't come back and be jailed or hanged, but he thought they were after his goods and they quarrelled and then he died last year. Which is why Master Alex is head of the family now and living in this Hall. Point is, after all that, there's a good many folk have good reason to keep their eyes on Hoghtons and what goes on in their houses, so you give them no occasion, right?
FULK Right.

WILL [*moving away a little, eyes to hearth*] Master Cottam says you have some other visitors.

ROGER Does he now? Well that's the other reason you keep quiet. There's plenty to do here with teaching the youngsters their music and writing for the revels and whatnot. And in case you're thinking, there's women enough here so you don't have to be down in the village all the time.

WILL Who is it we teach? Is it the master's children?

ROGER He's got none. Well, he's got one daughter out of wedlock, twenty something now, married to a man over in Charnock used to be cook here. [*Looks towards exit*] Poisonous bitch. You don't need to know except to keep out of her way. No, there's the children of the gentry on this estate and the next one or two, that get sent here for their nurture, nine of them last time I counted, Woottons, Savages, Pembertons.

WILL [*turning*] And the other visitors? Do they come here to... teach as well?

ROGER Don't be too sharp for your own good. Ay, they come, and they have things to say, and the less *you* have to say about them the better. There's one coming next week. Master Hastings. Belongs to the Company, if that means anything to you.

FULK What Company's that?

WILL Do you not know? We had them back home. It's the priests overseas, they call themselves the Company of Jesus, the Society of Jesus, and they make this promise to –

ROGER I *said*, don't be too sharp. What the Company means for you and me is that from next week there'll likely be more eyes on this house than usual. So *you* watch and keep quiet. And if you recognise this man who's coming, this Hastings, you don't say a word, right? Now look, you'll find it strange these first days, specially you, Will, and they'll be laughing at your voice and what not, but don't fret and keep busy. Margery'll show you where you eat today and where you get your liveries and the rest [*stands; they follow suit*]. God keep you. I've to ride down to Ashcroft's with Rob and find out what happened to the bloody saltfish that's due [*Exit. Will and Fulk sit down again.*]

WILL You didn't tell me about your father.

FULK You were too busy telling me about yours. Cunning old bastard, your dad, by the sound of it.

WILL Yes. Yes. I don't know – what he thinks about all this. I think when Jack Cottam said I should go, he was glad, though. Glad to see the back of me for a spell.
FULK Why? Worried about you getting some lass – [*Will looks away*] Oh. Right. Leave it at that, shall we?
WILL Tell me about the plays in Chester.
FULK Did you have plays back where you come from?
WILL Only in Coventry. I never saw them, but my father did, and my aunt made some dresses for them sometimes. It's a while since they've been played there, though. You know. Popish.
FULK Aye, same in Chester. But me dad remembers how it was with the old Queen, when all the guildsmen went to Mass in the Abbey on Whitmonday around five in the morning, and the carts started up and the Rows sounded like a thunderstorm with it all, and you stood and walked till near sunset, and ate in the streets and you could see the ones you fancied twice or three times over [*stands and wanders towards front*]. And back home, the rooms were up to your armpits in cloth and leather, and me dad and mam would be up all hours stitching and embroidering for the guilds that asked them. Your auntie must have been the same, then, up all hours and the rest. Were you ever with her?
WILL Don't think she and my father got on. But he talked about her sometimes; talked about the plays a bit, too. Biggest day in the year, he'd say.
FULK Aye, same as me dad says. There was three days off work with it all. They say now you have to call it the midsummer plays, on account of there being no Corpus Christi any longer, I don't understand any of that, but last time it was still – well, still mostly what it was, for a while longer anyroad, only no more plays about Our Lady on account of it being popish, like you say. Five years ago, it was; they tried to have the mayor put in jail because of it, but nothing happened. Folk wouldn't let them. [*pause; back upstage*] Know something else me dad used to say?
WILL [*a little amused*] Tell me.
FULK [*pause*] Funny thing, I never really thought on it till lately, but he used to say as how this was one day in the year when every soul in Chester had the same story to tell. I couldn't make much of that, 'cause all the guilds had different plays to show, but he said it was all one story, and this one day of the year it

was everyone's story, everyone's business. I thought, was it just that everybody had jobs to do in the same thing, you know, but he said, no, it were more than that. You look up there at the plays on the carts, he said, and what you see is you, you and your neighbours. 'Cause Adam and Eve, they're you, and Noah and Our Lady and Herod and Maudlin and all, it's you, it's you making a fool of yourself and you saying yes to God and you saying no to God and you trying to keep him away and, and... [*embarrassed*] aye, well, something like that.

WILL Like you've got them all inside you, inside your head and your guts.

FULK [*animated*] Aye, that's it, like they're all inside and then, sudden like, you see them all out there. Like a mirror. And you never knew.

WILL Will they do them again, the plays?

FULK [*shrugs, turns towards hearth*] Tell the truth, I don't know. Like I said, there's enough want it put down for popery, even if there's many as'll fight to have it still. But what I say is, what's popish about Adam and Eve and Herod and all those? There they are in the Bible. [*pause*] There they are inside and all, if me dad were right. Bits of what you're like. With only God knowing how it all fits together.

WILL Yes. There they are. Inside. [*stands, walks to join FULK at hearth*] So what happens if there's no play? What happens to all those folk inside?

FULK What d'you mean?

WILL Christ, Fulk. A man would burst open if he couldn't see what he was like, if he couldn't get his insides shown him before God or whatever. If he couldn't see all that on the pageant, played out in front of him in this... mirror, like you said, and he could say, Yes, that's *me*, someone's seen me, someone's known what it's like, I exist. I'm here, not just in my head, but here for God and man and... He'd burst open like – like a man on the scaffold, like a man with his insides being, being... [*shivers*]

FULK [*startled*] Steady, Will. It's only plays we're talking of.

WILL Course. It's only plays.

[*Blackout*]

Scene III

[*MARGERY, THOMASIN, ALICE, SUSANNA – all late teens or early twenties – in foreground, other servants in background, talking*]

THOMASIN Which one, then?
MARGERY Give over. They've not been here a week, hardly.
THOMASIN Come on, Marge; you've seen more of them than we have.
ALICE How much more is what I'd like to know [*laughter*].
MARGERY God you're dull, you lot. Only one thing to talk about.
THOMASIN And the young lad from down south isn't dull? More things to talk about? Or is it more things than talking?
SUSANNA If you ask me, he doesn't fancy ladies. I reckon he's got his eye on Fulk.
MARGERY Don't be filthy, you stupid slut.
SUSANNA Oh! You know better, do you?
MARGERY He's all right.
THOMASIN No more than that?
MARGERY Like I said, it's less than a week, for Christ's sake! Anyroad, he'll come and go... [*laughter*] Oh God, shut up, you can't say anything with you, can you?
SUSANNA So what do you know about this one that's arrived now? Must be something special that we've all been told to come and greet him like this.
MARGERY I heard Roger say there was something special. That he's a priest with the Company, whatever that is, and the agents will be after him 'cause he's been around in the south and stirred it up.
SUSANNA Stirred it up? Do you mean he's for the King of Spain or something?
MARGERY I don't know, do I? I can't think Master Alex would have him here if he was a proper traitor.
THOMASIN Agents don't know the difference, though, do they? That's the point. I tell you straight, I don't fancy this. I don't want to be in front of the justices answering questions about whether I've been at Mass and being told I'm a traitor to the Queen if I have.
SUSANNA Will we all have to go, then? To Mass? And confess and all?

ALICE He won't have time to confess you. He's only here three weeks [*laughter*].
SUSANNA Straight, though? Do we go? Does the whole house go? What do I tell Sir Philip at the parish?
MARGERY You tell Sir Philip nothing, right? like as usual. Not that the old pillock'll notice any different, even if he's sober for a change. You tell nobody outside this house anything, no names, no times, no places. You act dumb. Shouldn't be difficult. [*Susanna swings at her and there is a short scuffle*]. Oh God, behave yourself, look it's Master Alex. And that must be him. Christ, he knows how to dress for a priest!

[*Alex has emerged at the top of the stairs, Hastings with him, a middle-aged man dressed in the height of fashion. Roger emerges from the knot of servants and bangs his staff for silence*]

ALEX [*awkward*] Right. God keep you. You're here to listen to Mr Hastings, who's our guest these next few weeks. But before he talks: you don't speak of him if you're asked down in the village except to folk you know for sure are our own people. If Sir Philip asks anything, Mr Hastings is my cousin returned from the Low Countries and he trades in jewels. The rest he'll tell you.
HASTINGS [*very formal and stately*] Masters, brother and sisters, thank you: you are generous to a stranger and a stranger who may bring bad things to this house. You all know it as well as I know it, and I shan't make sport with you by pretending it's otherwise. Yet it is indeed jewels I trade in. I am a priest of the Holy Roman Church and a brother of the Society of Jesus [*murmurs in audience*]. If I hide this from the world, I don't hide it from you, because for you, as the Lord says, I open my treasury and bring out things new and things old, and to you I offer a pearl of great price. Why then do I hide it from the world? For fear of the pains it may bring me? They are terrible to contemplate and I do fear them; I pray each day to be spared – not from the pains but from any fear that would make me false. No: I hide this because your neighbours who do not share the gift of faith with you and me, if they knew me for who I am would step further into error and sin by hating what they saw. For your neighbours believe men such as me to be traitors to our sovereign and our land. They believe us to be idolaters and

liars, and so, as the Lord says in his gospel, they think that by killing us they do a good deed. Shall I drive them into this folly and blasphemy? No. I hide who I am for love of them, until such day may come as they can truly know what I am and welcome it. [*walks down a few steps, spreads hands*] So you, you must share this love and share this secret. For from you I hide nothing. I dress like a worldly man and perhaps you will hear me speak like a worldly man, but you will know that this is only playing. You know that I am here for one thing alone and that is to make and keep you reconciled to Holy Church and steadfast in your religion until God opens the eyes of our neighbours and our governors.

So may God keep you all faithful. Tomorrow morning at five and every morning when I am here I shall offer the Holy Sacrifice in the upper parlour and I urge you all to be present. If you need to make your duties tomorrow and to receive the Body of the Lord, I shall be in my chamber tonight after six, ready to hear your confessions. Remember: if my life depends on your silence, your salvation depends on my liberty to speak while I am here. God save you and God save our sovereign Lady. [*He and Alex withdraw, to a buzz of comment*].

ROGER Now then: back to your work. Off with you; back to work straight and you may have less to tell Mr Hastings in your confessions. [*laughter as they drift off*]

SUSANNA So am I safe then if I go to Mass? Nobody tells, right?

MARGERY Nobody tells. Nobody tells anyone outside the household except that we have a jewel merchant here who's kin to Master Alex. And outside the household means Mistress Crichlow and all. She'll go to the Sheriff soon as wink.

THOMASIN [*half-laugh*] God you're scaring me.

SUSANNA Nobody tells, they won't know. [*Will and Fulk fall in with them*]

WILL They know already. The agents know where all the priests are.

THOMASIN What do you mean? Do you mean we're all going to be taken and put to the question? I'm off if that's it, I'm off.

WILL Calm down. They know but they don't need to do anything. They like you to know that they know, that's all, to keep you scared. But they won't take you or anyone unless it's time to let them in London know they haven't gone to sleep. And the further we are from London, the slower they get.

SUSANNA How do *you* know, anyroad?

WILL I saw a bit back home. They bide their time till there's talk of treason in London, then they look for a few to catch and serve up to the Sheriffs. And maybe then they have a good quartering to look forward to, and everyone can feel safe.

MARGERY Good Christ! Are you trying to cheer us up or what?

WILL [*shrugs*] It's where we are. Safer here than down in the Midlands because the justices here don't fancy killing their kin, from all I hear. And no-one fancies killing servants, so you can settle yourself. They don't need your evidence to hang a man.

FULK Don't let him frighten you. We all go to Mass with closed eyes so we've seen no-one there, and we keep the rest inside. I don't say it's easy, but it's all we can do; and if some silly fool goes and leaves the household suddenly, that's one thing as'll draw the agents and the Sheriffs here in no time, so we stay and keep our counsel.

WILL Right enough. Shut up the doors and light the torches. There's hard winter nights out there. [*The women leave, with one or two backward looks*]

FULK Will, you soft bugger. Do you want to keep them up all night panicking each other into convulsions?

WILL They know what it's like. And if they don't, they need to learn. When the priests come, everything changes, all the words mean something different, no-one's name is their own. You learn your words and if you forget, you don't know what'll follow. They need to know that.

FULK Come on. There've been priests through here times enough before, if what they say is right.

WILL Of course.

FULK You're not convinced.

WILL I'm not convinced. Old Roger thought I might know him. I do. Not just any priest, Mr Hastings. I met him down south; he had another name then. And Jack Cottam said he was one that the Queen herself would give a fortune to get taken.

FULK God. Do you reckon they know, Master Alex and all them?

WILL They will soon enough. Christmas games, Fulk, Christmas games. We'd better start learning our songs.

[*They go off. Blackout*]

Scene IV

[*WILL alone, with wine-cup, on a heap of playing cloths; sound of singing and loud conversation off stage. MARGERY comes in, a bit drunk, sits down near him; silence for a moment, then –*]

MARGERY They want you. They want another song.

WILL Let them want.

MARGERY Don't be like that. They love hearing you sing. We all love hearing you. We all love you, Will, some of us more than others [*small giggle*]. Are you going to be kind to us? Are you going to be kind to me [*hand on his arm*]? It'll be Lent tomorrow; you can make the most of it tonight.

WILL Kind? Is that what it is?

MARGERY Tired of your rough northern company indoors, are you?

WILL No. No, it's... [*pause*]

MARGERY What?

WILL I can't hear. When there's a crowd like that, I can't hear.

MARGERY You can't hear what? You've got two ears like the rest of us, haven't you?

WILL I can't hear what they're saying. I can hear the noises, but I can't... hear inside my head. I can't hear where the noises come from. I can't... God. I can't...

MARGERY For God's sake, Will. [*Pause*] All right. Shall I go?

WILL Do what you like. Go back to where people are *kind*.

MARGERY I like being here. I like being with you. I want to listen to you. Even when you're as mad as you are now. [*Pause*] Some of them think you fancy me. [*Pause; awkwardly*] I didn't know. Some of them think you fancy Fulk. I don't... I don't know how I can tell –

WILL God. [*Suddenly flaring*] God! It's a game with you, isn't it? It's a stupid bloody game with all of you. You think – Christ, I don't know – you think it's about *fancying*, like you fancy a meat pie or a new coat? Something you put on you. Something you put inside you. You don't know anything. Anything. I've heard women say it: I want you inside me, they say. And I want... [*thinks; change*] yes, I want to be inside, yes, I do, I want to be in there, hearing where it all comes from, where it all... And sometimes, whether it's a man or a ...

MARGERY Do you fancy Fulk?

WILL For God's sake! No! Is that what they're saying? [*desperately*] How do I know? Do I want him inside me, do you mean? Me inside him? Yes, I want to know how I get to listen to where he comes from. I think of him for hours, how I can hear who he is. God, I think of you for hours, too. You, all of you... [*fast, confused*] That's what happens, you know, when people meet. They want to be inside each other but they're frightened to have someone else inside them because you know what its like? Do you know what it's like for a man when someone wants to be inside him and you're stabbed through like a trophy, like something you bring back from the day's hunting? I've been... Ah God, I can't...

MARGERY [*Backing away a bit; not knowing what to say*] Stop it, Will. I don't know anything about that. Don't talk past me. It's me here; not Fulk, not whatever man you... and not any woman from down South. It's *me* that can't hear... I don't know how what to make of you when you go on like this. I can't think... But you know what it is to... to want to come into a woman... to..?

WILL [*Savagely*] I want to be in you. I want to be where I can hear you from way up inside your gut. I want to hear where you speak from. [*Pause*] Perhaps I want that with Fulk too. Like you said when you were joking with your *friends*. [*Quieter*] I don't know. All I know is I can't hear when you're all there, all making your game, your barley-breaks and your... your... I want to be away from the noise. I want to be away from the wanting too. I don't want to go carrying bodies away from the hunting, jabbed through with a spear like, like hares or moles or, or...

MARGERY Oh for God's sake, Will. Can't you be quiet now and just... [*touches him again, nervously*]

WILL [*pulls away*] What? Be quiet and what? Do you think I can just quietly slip into you and say sugared things and slip out again and no wounds left, no traces on the skin...

MARGERY Is it Father – Mr Hastings?

WILL Is what Hastings? Do I want to be inside him?

MARGERY My God, Will! You're as filthy as the girls. I mean – you spent all that time with him when he was here before, you used to hang on the edge of all that talk I can't understand. You used to listen to him as if your life depended. Is that what you

want, to go off with him, to go overseas and be a priest and, and – then there's no more of all this, and...
WILL And get the executioner inside my own guts and groping for my heart? That would fit, wouldn't it? The end of a man who wanted to be inside other people. Poetic whatever. No. It isn't Hastings. He listens, though. He can hear in a crowd. He's not interested in being kind either, not to anyone. I think he listened to me. I think he listened to something I can't hear inside myself. But I don't know if that means I have to speak what he wants to hear. He doesn't know what I'm saying now. He doesn't know what it is to want like this.
MARGERY [*Quietly*] Whatever you want, Will; whatever you want. If you tell me to go, I'll go.
WILL Don't go. [*Pause*] I don't know where you are now, but I don't want you anywhere else. Don't go.

[*She puts out her hand. He begins to pull at her dress, uncertainly at first, then hard; kisses her savagely. She wriggles away. They face each other for a moment, then she stands and backs towards exit, beginning to unlace her dress. Blackout. The music outside fades and is replaced by something different, liturgical – Tallis, 'In jejunio et fletu', for example, or a Byrd Kyrie.*]

The light comes up on the upper stage, showing Hastings, in vestments, with the ceremonial bowl of ashes for the liturgy of Ash Wednesday: a handful of figures approach; to each one he says the formula, 'Remember you are dust and to dust you will return'.

Will enters, carrying his shirt, downstage left. Hastings turns, meets his eye; locks eyes, pauses. Will turns away and exits; Hastings continues. Lights fade.]

Scene V

[*Evening, late spring. ALEX with WILL; papers on the table*]

ALEX Good. It'll be as good a Whitsun as we can manage in these times. Two interludes?
WILL Two. Mr Hastings thought we should have the second. I think it's something he wrote.

ALEX Aye. [*Flat*] He says he used to write plays for the Emperor's court when he was overseas. Not that I said that, Will. You don't know who he is. And you don't know where he's been since he was here last.

WILL Of course. I don't know who he is.

ALEX Long way from the Emperor to here, eh? [*Looks at papers*] I'm not too sure he's measured the miles if this is anything to judge by. Still and all. I'll not deny him the pleasure. He's here to keep us up to the mark. [*Pause*] Has he talked to you?

WILL Once or twice. Not for long.

ALEX I think he's got his eyes on you. You know what I mean and what I don't. There's a good few have gone overseas for religion, Will, my own brother among them and your Jack Cottam's brother and all, and I can't make my mind up about it. Can't see much to hope for here in England, even if I wasn't coming to the end of my time. What I can see, Elizabeth Tudor's set for a long haul, and if she's not wed yet, chances are she'll never wed, whatever they say. And if she doesn't wed, there's nothing as'll make her change her mind on religion. If I was her, I don't know as I would myself, what with all these silly buggers running round with the King of Spain and the Queen of Scots and God knows who. So I can see why a young man who wanted to practice his religion properly might travel, even set up with one of these seminaries or with the Society. What I can't make out is why they come back and put us all in the way of the gallows and the knife. Shouldn't say this, I dare say. I know the man's here for our good, and it's a comfort to have the sacrament and all. But it strains a man's heart to be always looking over his shoulder and watching his words and – wearing masks. Christmas guising all year round but damn all pastime in it.

WILL Perhaps... perhaps there's nowhere now... [*stands, moves away*]

ALEX Eh?

WILL ... nowhere to be simple. Nowhere where you don't have to watch your words and wear your masks. [*Abstractedly, gradually forgetting Alex*] Watch your words. You watch them like birds clustering and forming up for winter, or coming in to land or sitting so still on the trees you'd think they were wood or leaves, and all the time they're breathing, quick, soft, ready to spring up and fly, and you can't net them or bring them down with fowling-pieces and you can't get them where you want them...

ALEX Will. What the hell are you talking about?
WILL Sorry, Master Alex. Only it seems everywhere you go you have to make choices now that people didn't. You can – see words out there, all the different ways you could talk, all the different ways you could make sense of the world, nothing fixed, and you in the middle of it, whirling round and trying to catch a glimpse of something, something that's really there, only all the little dances and masquings of people talking to each other are hiding it and – and you have to feel the stream running under it all, like, I don't know...
ALEX [*Deadpan*] Much more of this and I'll be sending you overseas myself to get a bit of peace around her instead of listening to you rabbiting on like that. Anyroad, don't you go yet awhile, Will, all right? I can't see you in a black frock in the Low Countries, and I don't fancy seeing you in red trimmings on the butcher's block either. That second interlude's fine; we'll cope. What about the music for the first one? We have the two viols, but where we get five extra singers I don't... [*Door opens, ROGER enters, flustered*]
ROGER Sorry master. Mistress Crichlow, and she won't be gainsaid.
ALEX God. All I need. Well, let her come. [*Roger leaves*] Will, we'll see each other in the morning about the rest of it.
WILL Master [*bows and begins to move. MARGARET (MEG) CRICHLOW pushes past him as she comes in*]. Mistress.
MEG [*to Alex*] Who's this?
ALEX Will Shakeshafte. You've seen him here before. He's with us from down south for a spell to help with the playing and the music.
MEG You mean he's another papist vagabond you're looking after and risking all our lives and goods. Perhaps you need to remember that your property's not yours for much longer and if you put it at jeopardy we'll all suffer.
ALEX Thank you, Meg. Do you know, I'd forgotten I was dying. Will, off you go.
MEG Wait for me below.
ALEX Since when do you give orders to my people?
MEG Since you started showing you're not fit for the governance of your own goods. [*To Will*] Go. [*He leaves*]
ALEX You know how to make yourself welcome, Meg. What do you want?

MEG I need to know what you've done for us.
ALEX What I'm leaving you, you mean?
MEG Yes. [*Sits*] We've a chance of buying Moss Side mill at Charnock. We need to know whether it's going to be a quarter of the property we'll have or more. We need to know this week.
ALEX Christ, Meg. Can't you wait a few months? This is hard, even for you.
MEG Even for me? Do you want me to pretend I've come to pay a kind visit to my ailing old dad so that we can remember the happy days of childhood?
ALEX Come on, Meg. Your mother had a house and a good marriage to Beesley. It's not that you were left in a ditch with her.
MEG I might as well have been. And you never knew what life in Beesley's house was like. Thank God for Walter. He's a fool but he leaves me alone.
ALEX Don't start on that again. I can't say anything about what Beesley did or didn't. I didn't know then and I don't know now.
MEG You've always known what you chose to know. Anyroad, I'll not waste time in that. What can you tell me?
ALEX [*angry*] Why should I tell you anything? You want my goods, you might try and make a friend of me.
MEG A friend? God help us. Too late for that. And I'm not likely to make a friend of a known papist in these times.
ALEX You're still deep in with those bloody Puritan fools or whatever they call themselves now in Preston? Shaking the tree to see what more fruit you can get to fall. As if there wasn't enough already, lying on the grass and stinking because of you and your like, talking about reforming religion all over again.
MEG Why should you tell me? What would you say if I said I was going to the Sheriff to talk about your guests?
ALEX I'd say you always were a bitch but I didn't reckon you were a traitor.
MEG Traitor? You have the gall to talk about traitors when there's enough traitors in your attics to hang the whole household.
ALEX [*Rising, very controlled; takes her wrists*] If you talk like that again, I don't care what you say to the Sheriff. Fleetwood's not a complete fool and he knows malice when he sees it and he's enough left of the old loyalties to his friends not to leap on his horse to London and fetch the agents. You try that, Mistress, and you'll not get even a quarter. You'll get my curse and a

pennorth of rope to hang yourself if one of my people doesn't get to you first.
MEG [*Equally cold, shaking off his hands*] I need to know. You'll not threaten me out of my rights.
ALEX You'll know soon enough. Now you need to leave. I'm a sick man, Meg, not just to spite you but because I am, and I need to go to my rest. Roger! [*Roger opens door*]
ROGER Master.
ALEX Mistress Crichlow is leaving. I'm for my bed. [*Walks upstairs heavily and silently*]
MEG I told that lad to wait. I need to speak with him.
ROGER You'll speak with him outside this house, not here. This isn't yours yet, and God grant it never will be.

[*MEG strikes him across the cheek. He stands still for a moment, then takes her by the arm, very hard. She winces.*]

ROGER [*Face close up to hers*] Not yet, Mistress. [*He pushes her away and walks off. She stumbles, recovers herself, crosses the stage from the foot of the stairs. Light comes up on Will, seated, waiting*]
MEG [*breathing hard*] Come with me. Now.

[*Meg and Will exit together*]

Scene VI

[*MARGERY comes in, followed by FULK*]

MARGERY [*flatly, arms tightly clasped*] No.
FULK I don't know, Marge, I only hear what they're saying. He's not – well, he's not just pretending with you, I know that. He's not one of those lads that, you know, talks himself into bed and then buggers off. And she...
MARGERY No. He's been in her bed all right, I don't need anyone to tell me that. And you know why? Because he thought, 'What'll it be like to be in her bed? I've got to know, I've got to know what it's like to be a betrayer, to know I've got another woman.' I suppose it's the same with whatever poor cow he's got back in the South, I never asked about her. And you know something else? I think he asked himself, 'What'll it be like to

be in bed with a bitch who's going to betray me and all? What's it like to play with a woman who could give us all into the Sheriff's hands if she wanted? Who hates her father and everything to do with him? He wanted to live in another world for a bit, that's what. He wanted to live in a world where there's no promises and no kindness and no, no... [*She chokes on her words for a moment. Silence*]

FULK I'm sorry.

MARGERY Much use to me.

FULK No, but I am.

MARGERY [*Sits*] You don't see it, do you? You think he's like you, you poor sod. Or like me. You stand there, I stand here, and what I see, I see. And him, he wants to stand there and stand here and look out of your eyes and mine and – hers. Only you can't do that, can you? You can't step out of your skin? He hates living in his skin, I know that. In bed. It's like I can hear him rolling around inside his skin as if he were tossing round under the sheets when they get too hot. He says less and less to me, you know. Only when it comes to it, he bites and pushes more and more, God help me. Christ, Fulk, I feel I've been eaten alive. And now –

FULK He was never going to stay, was he? I mean, you must have known he wasn't going to stay?

MARGERY I don't know. I thought there was something I could do [*Laughs harshly*] God, that sounds pathetic. How many women do you suppose hear themselves saying *that*? I thought... [*pauses*] I thought I might stop him going off overseas and risking his bloody life with Hastings and them. [*Turns her back to Fulk; muffled*] I thought it was God I had to worry about. Not Mistress bloody Crichlow.

FULK [*Walks to hearth, leaning on settle*] Well, say he has been... been with her. You know her. She doesn't *want* him. Not, you know, *him*. She wants to know what it's like and all, I reckon, what it's like to take what you see, take it in your father's face and... your God's. She's a walking itch, that woman, never rested, greedy for whatever's there because she's always been thrown the scraps. You get poisoned with scraps, I reckon, sooner or later.

MARGERY [*Looks at him with surprise, a half-smile*] My God, Fulk. Some things you do notice, then.

FULK Ay well... But if she has been with him, she'll not stay at it. What worries me is what she's going to get from him if she's minded. If she really wants to make life hell for her dad and everyone here.

MARGERY Like I said. Where she lives, there's no promises. She'd see Alex out of here on the moors in his nightgown tomorrow if she could. Christ. I think she'd see him on the scaffold without a blush. [*Stands, brushes herself down*] Do you reckon he's heard? Alex?

FULK Couldn't say. I'd be surprised if he hadn't, but you can't tell, specially not now he doesn't move out much. It still looks to me as if he trusted Will. I guess he'll be – bleeding a bit if he does know.

MARGERY Shouldn't he trust him? Do you really think she's pressing Will for something, something important?

FULK [*Pause, moves downstage*] I can't say much. Only Will does know something about Hastings. He saw him down south, he said once, only he had another name then. So maybe if she got wind... And if he didn't rightly know how much he was telling her or of he didn't see how set she was against her father...

MARGERY [*Sharp*] He's not a fool. And whatever I said, he's not going to send anyone to the scaffold if he can help it. I think – God, I think he'd feel the hangman's hands on his own body so much he couldn't do it, never mind anything else.

FULK [*turns back to her*] Do you think she knows about Hastings and the meeting tonight?

MARGERY I reckon. We're all bidden. He probably told her himself and all. Tell the truth. Strip the clothes off, strip the skin off. She won't come, though, and my guess is she'd be none the wiser if she did. You've heard Hastings. Talks like a man walking a rope: all obedience to the Queen's grace, no sedition, no word of criticism, nothing for the King of Spain to rub his hands over. All about returning to the truth that makes you free, so that nobody has to walk round in masks and disguises any more or come to Mass in the shadows with your cloak round you and your face hidden. [*Pause*] All very simple. Only it's not.

FULK Do you not think the old days will come again, then? Mass in the parish and Sir Philip's woman out of the parsonage and back with her sister, and the plays in Chester town and the monks back in the Abbey?

MARGERY Tell you something, Fulk, things don't come back. Haven't you seen that? Hastings lets folk think it's about the old days coming again, all the good things, the times when we were just ourselves. Only it was never like that. It never was simple. Perhaps we never were ourselves. Christ, I sound like Will now. But what Hastings will bring isn't the same, and there's new – choices and new, I don't know, new clothes to wear and new things to think. Once you know it *could* be different, it's all changed. [*Pause*] Like when you know your man's been in another bed. Things don't come back.
FULK I'm sorry.
MAREGRY You said that. [*Moves towards exit. Pause*] We go in an hour, is that right? Ashcroft's?
FULK Ashcroft's. There's folk coming up from Preston. Be a long night. Alex is coming and all, Roger's getting him ready, God help him.
MARGERY [*Pause*] I – used to joke about it, but I need to say. The girls and all. They used to... we used to say he fancied you too.
FULK Ay. I had heard.
MARGERY And?
FULK And nothing. [*Rallies*] Tell you something, though. You don't have to be in bed to think you're being eaten alive. You can eat a man by listening, did you know that? You can eat a man through his eyes. And you cannot know yourself, not know who you are by the time it's done. [*Silence*]
MARGERY I'm sorry.
FULK Much use to me. As they say. I'm going for my boots. [*Pause*] He wasn't ever going to stay.
MARGERY No.

[*They go off separately*]

Scene VII

[*ALEX, HASTINGS enter with ROGER and others, WILL hanging back. Cloaks, gloves, etc. removed. Alex and Hastings sit on settle by hearth, Roger pours wine, exits, Will sits on floor. First few exchanges as others drift off*]

ALEX Well. Well. Do you think the Queen's Grace will thank you for that?

HASTINGS The Queen's Grace may thank me or not as she pleases. I spoke my thoughts.

ALEX Did you?

HASTINGS I spoke my thoughts and they all listened hard. Look. You know and I know that she has no passions in matters of religion. She's shrewd, she's careful for her safety; she knows that when the ground moves under her, she must move with it or be swallowed up. Oh, I know there are fools who talk about war and invasion and calling on the King of Spain to sort it out, God help us; and there are – well, I can hardly call them fools, can I? – in Rome who speak very large about these things as well, as if some idiot's knife or bullet would put and end to... But fools is what they are. And I'm not, Alex, whatever else I am, nor is Elizabeth Tudor. If the ground moves... and it will, if enough of these folk believe they can find their way back to the old religion without blood and treason.

ALEX Good argument, maybe. But since when has she or anyone ruled by argument? She rules by...

HASTINGS She rules by show and high state, like every prince since the beginning of the world. I know: I've seen it, you've seen it. Princes are magicians, specially in these days when you can buy the sparkling toys and the machines to make people gasp. I saw it in Prague with the Emperor, poor softheaded soul. But –

ALEX But there you have it. You don't get a magician breaking his wand by choice. You don't get a player stepping away from the centre of the stage when he's in full spate. You've seen it, you've seen her. She loves that stage. They all love her on it...

HASTINGS But think of it. What if your players here came out in front of you with no lines learned? Never seen the parts they were to play? What if they'd never even seen a playbook? I tell you, this realm tore up the playbooks fifty years back and no amount of pageant and state and jewelled dresses and fine allegories and magical machines will make up for it. Come on: she knows that half the courts in Europe call her bastard or whore or both. She knows there's one thing she can't buy and flaunt like another jewel, and that's legitimacy, Alex, legitimacy. There's no lawful ground beneath her, no playbook to say she's speaking her part right. So she goes on spinning her webs for all she's worth, a spider furiously stitching up all the little broken twigs, with more and more little bodies hanging on the web. It's like what she wears, all the pearls hanging by little threads, all the lace so thin you could tear it with a fingernail. If you were she – if you were she, don't you think you might be ready, sooner or later, to trade all that, all the terror and the panic of an actor on stage with no part learned, no part written, would you not think of trading that for recognition? For the courts and the Pope to look on and say at last, yes, I know what she's saying, yes, this is a true performance, she knows her lines?

ALEX Ay well, like I say: she won't thank you for that! She won't relish being called a spider, and I dare say she loves her clothes and all. But you see, I'm not so sure about her, Edward: you can love all this even when it's panic and fear; you can be excited all the way up your virgin insides, if that's what they are. And whose recognition is it that matters? When all the courts in Europe have had their say, it's these folk here who see in her what they know and what they want. These are the ones she worries about at night, not some foreign papist holding his nose.

HASTINGS But if they, the ones she worries about, if they start to see that there's more that they want, there's more than she can give them maybe, if they see that she...

WILL [*awkward and louder than he meant*] Father. Can I... what...

ALEX [*startled*] Eh? God, Will, I thought you'd gone.

WILL No, I – listened, when you were talking back there, and then I...

ALEX What, then? Make sense to you?

WILL Oh it made sense. But only if - if you know, if you really know, so that you'd die for it, only if you know there really *is* a playbook. But what if there isn't? What if you really are pushed on that stage and no-one could have told you your lines anyway because, because there wasn't...

ALEX For Christ's sake, Will! You're not turning Lutheran?

WILL I'm not turning anything, sir. I want to know how you know the playbook's there, in Rome or wherever. Perhaps it's only what someone else did, what someone else said, hundreds of years ago, when they were on their own on a stage and there were no playbooks. And – you know spiders? They spin it out of themselves, don't they; they get it out of their bowels and...

HASTINGS What's in those bowels, though? You know your catechism. What's in any of us except lies and tales and images of who we are, that we set up and worship? God, these reformers are simple! As if idolatry were only bowing down to images and paintings, not bowing down to what you see in the mirror, what you find lodged at the back of your imagination. What comes out of that nothing that's in the heart?

WILL You want me to say 'nothing', I know. But I don't... I don't think it's like that. Perhaps you see just that: that you're nothing and there's only despair inside and so you have to – well, to look around and find someone else's eyes and find an earth and a heaven and...

HASTINGS A new heaven and a new earth out of your bowels, eh? That's a clever spider, Will, but I've not met any spiders except the ones that spin in the dark corners for a night or two and then get swept away. All right: speaking of a playbook may be a foolishness, because I know about plays and you and your friends do too, but I'm here to tell you, and all those folk there tonight, that there's something they can trust that isn't just their bowels and isn't even just their prince. [*pause: then, deliberately and unconvincingly light*] And if I didn't think that, d' you reckon I'd be risking my own bowels for it? Eh?

WILL [*silent*]

HASTINGS All right. It's late. Alex, you're three quarters asleep.

ALEX I'm four quarters confused, I'll tell you that.

HASTINGS Will: come back when you're ready. I still have some things you need to hear, whether you think so tonight or not. Help Alex to his bed.

WILL Yes. [*pause*] I don't make light of it, you know. I'm not mocking. The pains, I mean and what might...

HASTINGS [*turns away slightly*] All right. All right. I know what you mean and what you don't. Come back when you can take it.

[*Blackout*]

Scene VIII

[*MEG alone. WILL comes in, looks around*]

MEG No, just me. If they told you Margery was looking for you, I expect there was a mistake.
WILL What do you want? I can't tell you more. You know I can't.
MEG There's more to tell, then.
WILL You can twist my words as much as you like. I'm not pretending. There's no more.
MEG You know about twisting words, I dare say. This house is full of people busily twisting words. You could make a bloody bedcover out of all the plaiting and knitting-up and fancywork here. They say that, you know, about papists. You can't tell if they're atheists or double agents or treble because they give all their skill to making these patterns of words that cover up the plain things, cover up all the treasons and devices. Who knows what they are when they're not playacting?
WILL And you? Who knows what you are? So you've taken on the part of a rejected bastard, like the cheap stories they show in the innyard. The bastard plots for his inheritance and the husband gets cuckolded and the wife schemes for freedom and the servants get drunk. Don't tell yourself, don't tell me, you haven't decided who you're going to be. It's not a difficult part to play.
MEG Alex said you talked nonsense. You know what was done to me.
WILL I know what was done to you. Why does that make you who you are? You still have to choose what to do.
MEG Oh yes. So I do. So do you. I choose to stop arguing philosophy with you and you need to choose, you supposedly clever man, whether you want me again and what price you're ready to pay.
WILL I don't pay.
MEG Oh, very high-minded. You don't pay Margery, and you don't pay whatever whore you have back in the Midlands and you expect that women will never ask you. But some of us will, you know, some of us who don't reckon ourselves so lucky to have you in bed that we don't think of payment. Come on, Will. [*He is silent*] I tell you what, I'll help you put your hand in your pocket for me. You said you'd seen him before?

WILL Who?
MEG Hastings. You said you'd seen him.
WILL I never told you that.
MEG There's others can talk too. Don't lie. You'd seen him before. So. You're not what anyone would call a travelled man, so you saw him back in whatever sorry shitheap you lived on in the Midlands. So what connects that with here, that's the only question I've got left, because if I can answer that I'll have some information worth having. The only question is whether we both get something else along the way that might be worth remembering [*moves towards him*]
WILL [*flinching*] I've no more for you. I don't want any more... remembrances. [*shakes off hand on his arm*] I don't want you [*more and more harshly*]. I don't want you, I'm not going to betray anyone to keep your bloody inheritance safe. And if you think your father will give you what he's promised if you go to the Sheriff or the agents, you don't know him. He's not afraid of dying, but I tell you something else, if it comes to breaking faith with his God and his honour, he won't mind the rest of us dying either.
MEG He broke faith with his wife. That's why I'm here. I don't know whether he'll give me what I want, but I do know his faith's a little bit more fragile than you say. It's worth trying.
WILL He's your father. Wait; keep your thoughts to yourself, he'll do his duty by you. Try and force him and you'll have blood on your hands and nothing else in them.
MEG Do you know, I thought a shopkeeper's son might be easier to manage than a gentleman. You're as stupid as the rest of them when it comes to it, aren't you?
WILL He took me in when it was asked. He honoured his friendships. He's been good to me and to Fulk...
MEG And to Mr – Hastings So he was honouring friendships when he took you in. Thank you. So who does he count for a friend in the Midlands? [*pause*] Cottam; Jack Cottam of Tarnacre, went for a schoolmaster in – where was it? You're one of Cottam's boys, that's it. You won't tell me but it's no great matter to find it out. I knew you'd tell me something, Will, and I'm grateful. But not that grateful. That doesn't count as payment. [*caresses him in passing; Will stares at her*] So what shall I do with this little windfall? Once the Sheriff hears, he'll have to act,

whatever Alex says. He'll find out who the big men were among the papists who've been through the Midlands these last few months and he can do well out of it if they net one of the great fish. I dare say you've heard of Mr Campion? Edmund Campion? No? [*W. motionless*] Quite a story. They talk about it even in Preston, do my friends. He was at the Emperor's court, they say and now he's here, been in England a year or more, leaving his little pamphlets on the seats in churches and begging for a disputation with the scholars in Oxford to show off his learning and persuade them all back into error and darkness. Mr Hastings writes, doesn't he? Perhaps I might be persuaded by his scholarship, do you think, if I could see what he's been writing.

WILL You know nothing. Hastings is Hastings, that's all I know.

MEG Oh Will, you can do better than that. As you said: no-one is who they are. No one's name is their real name. I am not what I am, yes? What I want to know is who was it who decided to be Hastings and come here to bring deceit and sedition. And when I know that – well, I may find out a few other things about my father and his household. And my future. You know, you were right earlier and I was wrong. You don't know what was done to me. But you were right too. I choose who to be. And I do not choose to be a slave in my father's house or my foster-father's – or my heavenly Father's for that matter, if you understand anything about such things. [*Pause*] A pity you wouldn't pay. I thought it a fair bargain. [*exit, leaving Will alone in silence for a long moment*]

Scene IX

[*Late at night. HASTINGS in settle by the fire, in shadow, with wine, alone. Behind him the door opens and WILL slips in*]

HASTINGS It's no good, Will. [*Will starts*] You'll never make a servant in a great house. They know how to walk without noise.

WILL God, Father, you gave me a shock. What are you doing awake at this hour?

HASTINGS Come and drink some wine. What am I doing? I'd guess something different from what you've been doing at this hour. Meg or Margery? [*pushes bottle and cup towards Will*]

WILL What?

HASTINGS Meg or Margery? Or is there another I've missed? I hope it was Margery if I'm allowed any preference.
WILL Meg is... Father, Meg wants to know who you are so that she can use it to force her father –
HASTINGS Yes, it's all about her inheritance, no? Not a stupid woman, even if she's a murderous one. How much did you tell her?
WILL What do you mean?
HASTINGS Well, some women have a way of finding things out in bed. So they tell me. I wouldn't know, of course. My guess is that you told her more than you expected to. They tell me that happens in bed too. But it's no matter, I'm moving on the day after tomorrow. Back south. [*more quietly*] Things I need to finish there.
WILL What about the papers you...
HASTINGS I'll send for them or come back for them. You've looked at them?
WILL Yes.
HASTINGS Any clearer about where you'll be?
WILL [*longish pause*] I can't come with you.
HASTINGS Tell me.
WILL I can't. It's – it's not Margery or...
HASTINGS I didn't think so.
WILL Doesn't all that matter to you?
HASTINGS [*gets up impatiently, paces*] For God's sake Will! I'm not a first year novice in a nunnery. Men do what they do; if there's enough in them, they find out sooner or later how to keep out of bed with boys or women, once they know where they have to be. Don't you think I've seen worse than you and your friends, ten times over? You long for the game, then you need to come and confess it, then you'll do without it when you have to. And you – I know something of men like you, men who know that when they get out of bed, whether it's a boy or a woman, they feel they've spent something of their soul and the day comes when they don't want to waste it any longer. Is that right?
WILL [*low*] You know it is. But I said it isn't that. If I knew, if I knew that all this, what the Company does, bringing this country back to the old religion, if I knew that was the, the story, the one story that would bring it all together, yes, I'd be there, I'd be away from women and the rest, I could make sense of [*pauses*] –

HASTINGS The pains. You don't have to be tactful, Will; I think of it quite often, you know.

WILL Yes. But wherever I look, it seems there isn't one story. The old religion is the only, the only – picture of things that speaks to me, yes, but it's as if there were still voices all around me wanting to make themselves heard and they don't all speak one language or tell one tale, and all that – it would haunt me if I tried what you do, and it would make me turn away from the pains and the question, because I'd know that there'd always be more than the old religion could say and it still had to be heard...[*trails away*]

HASTINGS You remember a couple of weeks back, we talked about spiders. Spinning worlds out of their bowels. It's a good picture, Will, but it's not what gives you hope. [*sits again*] You may hear all these other voices. Do you think I don't? But it's not every voice that tells how things really are. 'Test the spirits', says Scripture. Oh yes, I can quote Scripture when I have to as well as any Lutheran or Disciplinarian and a damn sight better than poor old Sir Philip. Test the spirits: test the voices. Some will let themselves be drawn in to harmony and some won't; and the ones that won't you have to leave alone. God speaks harmony. It's one thing we do know, you and I, yes?

WILL Yes.

HASTINGS Music talks to us, it tells us how it all should be, as if it's God's hint to us of what he purposes, and when we talk and write, we think music is where we should be and music is what we should sound like. And there's a cost to that. Not every voice comes in. I preach sermons about the saved and the lost, we all do. And when you get past the noise of parsons shouting, what's that about? Some voices are going to be out of tune for ever. Leave them, don't seek them out. They'll soften your heart in all the wrong ways and you'll forget that there's a truth at all.

WILL But what if they're – shut out of the harmony because no-one's let them be heard? What if the only way to... this harmony you talk about is like letting God bring it about when every human spirit has its voice. So what *you* thought was harmony turns out to be less than what God can do? And for that to happen, you've got to listen to the ones that are – like you said – 'out of tune'?

HASTINGS So you get to stand in for God meanwhile, is that it, conjuring spirits out of the deep in great armies so that the harmony is bigger and deeper than Mother Church can guess? You get to put us all straight and show us how small our world is? Brave thought. I shan't call it arrogant, because I don't think that's what you are, Will. But God gave his Church firm guidance, he gave us fathers and teachers, the creeds and the Pope and all of us priests, however stupid and sinful we are, because human hearts aren't made for endless welcome to all the voices there might be out there. [*Will starts to speak*] No, shut up, Will, I want to hear what I'm going to say, because I'm not sure I know myself where I'm going. [*Pauses; a half-smile*] The air's full of noises, full of spirits, and some send you mad, so you can't tell what's real from what's not. Truth, Will; that's what we're fighting about. I hate the Lutherans and the Calvinists and your half-witted Puritans in this ramshackle Church here, but there's one thing I don't hate about them and that's that they know they're fighting for truth. They're wrong about it, but they know it matters; and they don't shrink from the pains of the gallows and the block either.

WILL So theirs are the voices you shut out?

HASTINGS We have to. The devil has his choirs as well, and they can make you think for a moment that there's harmony there, or that there might be, but it's a song of the sirens. It's shipwreck that way.

WILL But... once you choose which voices you listen to, once you decide what clothes to wear, what beliefs to put on in the morning, how can you say that one of them is truth?

HASTINGS [*face to the fire, quite quietly*] You don't *choose* like that. You [*glances at Will, then back to fire*] – what do I say to you? – you surrender to the harmony you hear, you don't make it up, you don't write it like a tale or a fable out of your – [*smiles*] well, out of your bowels, as you elegantly put it.

WILL And what if you just can't help hearing more all the time? If what's asking you to surrender is just... well, bigger than what you and the others say, bigger than the harmony *you* can imagine? It's not that I want to make up the world out of my bowels. That was a foolish way of talking. I know I have to listen and when I listen I have to surrender. But, but I don't know what it is that I submit to, not as if I was surrendering to you or the

Pope – or the Archbishop or John Calvin or some mad Puritan clerk at Cambridge.

HASTINGS [*pauses, quite long*] All right. So this isn't the time when it's clear. All right, Will, I don't want you with me if you can't hear this, if you can't catch the harmonies. Because you're right, you're going to be asking every moment, have I heard right, have I heard enough, and that's not the state of mind that holds you upright on the scaffold. But what is there here for you? This nation is a sad place, people seizing what they can and shouting loudly about their freedom, Elizabeth Tudor painting her face and looking around for a mirror and not knowing from one day's end to the next what the world is except her theatre where she has to keep you all entertained, because when she stops entertaining you she'll die and so will you. Do you seriously reckon you or anyone can hold up the other kind of mirror to her now that'd show her the truth?

WILL [*slowly*] What if you could? What if you could make her say, This is me?

HASTINGS Don't hold your breath. How would anyone do that, now it's all gone, the feasts and the saints and the Mass itself? Because those are the real mirrors, that's where you look to see who you are. Look, you've heard what I hope for and what I don't, and I mean it. I hope she can be spoken to, that something will get through that great web she's woven and let the light in. But I know – well, I know at this time of night, anyway – the chances are pretty small. I know you can't just bring it all back in a night, the feasts and the abbeys and the pilgrims. I know whatever comes will be different. Perhaps after all the killings it'll be – I don't know, quieter or something. Because there'll be plenty more deaths – mine, probably, and your schoolmaster's brother and a few more, and the Society will go on sending us and the Queen will go on killing us. [*Pause; he gets up to walk downstage*] Here, in this nation, if you're not with us you're against us – more Scripture for you. But if you're not in with the ones who want the old religion, who is there, what is there? An endless servile dance around an ageing courtesan. The old ways falling apart and poor men abandoned on the roads and the people's wealth streaming into the hands of the Queen's favourites, and buying ships and guns for stupid, stupid wars...

WILL I can't tell, Father. And the guns and the wealth and the courts – are you telling me the Catholic courts are any better? You ought to know. What with the emperor and all. It's not as if this is the only sad nation in Christendom. What if we're all doomed to be sad now, sad and stupid? What if there's no way back to the old ways, if they ever were what we say they are? And the only thing now is to try and find room for the sadness to be – to be *there*, to be in front of your eyes and in your ears, so, so you know you're, I don't know, not asleep.

HASTINGS So you go back to the Midlands, you get some lass with child, you marry and take over the business, and you look and listen for all this when you have time to spare from the children and the merchandise and filling up your barns with grain to sell off dear when there's a bad harvest? There are plenty of things to make you deaf after a while.

WILL Perhaps. Perhaps on my deathbed I'll think, you know, he was right, that Father – Hastings, I'll think, hell, I've got it all wrong. Or perhaps I'll have forgotten what to listen for by then.

HASTINGS [*looks at him hard*] Not quite that, I think. I don't think you forget things. But remembering them won't come easy for you. So I don't know what you'll do with all this, Will. I don't know where you put it. I just pray you don't bury it. Ask yourself.

WILL [*Pause*] You leave the day after tomorrow?

HASTINGS I do. If I don't see you tomorrow, Will, you have my blessing for all the God-knows-what that you're going to do and my prayers that somehow or other you won't forget whatever it is we've been saying, and at this hour of the night I don't know any more than you what *that* is. [*Pause; slight smile*] And if the harmony ever starts up, you know where to find the brethren. Even if you won't find me. Give me a prayer when you can. I'll be needing it.

[*They stand. Silence. Will quickly kisses Hastings' hand. They go out by separate exits*]

Scene X

[ALEX *in his bed, visibly weak; ROGER, THOMAS*]

ALEX Will he talk?
THOMAS People do. I know he's a brave man, they mostly are, but once the experts have got to work, they'll get something, even if he doesn't know what he's told them.
ALEX So how long do you reckon we've got?
THOMAS Far as I know, they took him three or four days back. So it could be a week or two, depending who wants to talk to him. Did you know he was that big a fish? Been putting the universities in a fit as well as the court ever since he landed, by the sound of it.
ALEX Ay, well; he told me a bit, did Edward – Edmund, I should rightly call him, I suppose. The Emperor's court and all that. Young Will knew something too, he'd come across him back home, he said once, when he was using another name. And he knew about the Emperor.
ROGER Will knew something?
ALEX That's right. Why?
ROGER [*Awkward*] I'm sorry. I've got to ask.
ALEX Margaret, right?
ROGER Ay. Margaret. I did wonder.
ALEX You can go on wondering. I trusted him, and I think I was right. Don't trust his judgement, though, letting himself get caught by her. Cause I never trusted her, and I was right there and all. But God knows what she got from him and how. Like you say, Tom, they don't know what they're telling sometimes when they start in with the instruments. I reckon it's easier getting men out of the Tower in London than when they're set on some woman who's going to have their guts out in the other way. God knows why men go for it. I'd have spared him that, but I couldn't find the...
THOMAS It's true they had something on Edward from here. They knew who he was when they followed him down to Berkshire. And the only one who'd want to talk from round here is Meg.
ALEX She's already called. Roger saw her this morning.

ROGER [*To Thomas*] Ay. She wanted to speak to Master Alex and I wouldn't have it, I told her where to go. If she's going round with her own version of the rack or the needles, I'm not having him troubled, not now. But she made it clear enough who we'd got to thank for the news.

ALEX Roger wants me to die in peace, God bless him [*Roger pulls away angrily*]. I dare say she wants me to die and all, whether in peace or not. And I'm with her there. There's nothing to do now for Edward – Edmund, I should say – or Tom Cottam except pray. There's the will, though.

THOMAS Signed and settled?

ALEX Signed and settled, four weeks back, after he went off south. In case. And the two lads go to you if you'll have them, to Heskeths if you won't. [*Thomas tries to interrupt*]. No, don't say anything, you don't have to decide till things get clearer. Till I've gone, anyway. So long as it's there and you know it. Where they go from you or Hesketh and when, that's up to you.

THOMAS What about Meg?

ALEX That's what I wanted you both for. If I'd known all this for sure four weeks back – I guessed she would if she could, but I didn't know. Couldn't know till he was taken. She gets nothing, right? I want you as witnesses. Whatever's written down there, she gets nothing, and she'll have to go to law with you both sworn against her if she tries anything on. Problem?

THOMAS No problem. But you could get the lawyer and straighten it all out on paper.

ALEX No. [*With effort*] Lawyer comes, sees what's there, and if I don't die in a week or two there's plenty of time for him to let her know. He's closer in there with that Puritan lot than he lets on. So she finds out, there's time to make mischief for me and all of you. And the lads and all. Do it this way, with you swearing to what I said, and anything she says is going to sound like malice. You can drop a hint or two to the Sheriff about her and Will, and they'll think I'm getting back at her and they'll not want a thrown-off mistress tying up the law for months. If I change it and she sees it, she sees the plans for Will and Fulk, and she'll have grounds for setting them on to the two of them. As things stand, the will's made before anyone gets arrested or hanged, nothing suspicious you can put your finger on in law. No, she can wait, so long as you two will swear. Let her think I

was afraid to cross her, let her think she's going to get what she asked. And with good luck, the lads will have moved on by then.
ROGER Will won't stay up here. Fulk'll go back to Chester, I reckon, but Will..
ALEX Nothing doing with Margery, then.
ROGER [*Laughs shortly*] Christ, you don't miss much, do you? She'll get over it and nothing to show.
ALEX Nothing to show, eh? All these months with Edward and Will and Fulk and the rest and nothing to show. No wounds on the body, is that it? Everything under the skin and life goes on. For some. Everything out of sight under the skin; or is it under the playing clothes? [*Pause*] Well. Off you go. If I'm going to die in peace, Roger, I'd as lief not do it just this afternoon to oblige you. I need to sleep. [*They begin to leave*]. I'll see Will and Fulk in the morning. You can tell them. [*Pause*] God help us. Bloody times.

[*Blackout*]

Scene XI

[*Much activity, servants folding bedlinen, etc. MARGERY enters, obviously distressed, shaking off ROGER's hand*]

MARGERY I told them, I bloody told them, I said, he's not twenty-four hours dead, I said, how can you come in here and expect us to turn inside out for you, and they just, they just... One of them said, 'Well, he's in luck, then', and he said, that's more than I can say for the rest of you...
ROGER I know. It's how some of them do business, these agents. Like no-one's ever told them you need to behave like human beings when there's birth and death and stuff around. I know you did your best, love. Have they all gone?
MARGERY Thank Christ, yes. I tell you, Roger, if they'd stayed much longer I'd have had the kitchen cleaver out, and so would the rest of them. [*Pause. Breathes hard and collects herself.*] How much trouble is it, Rodge? Really?
ROGER Alex did his best. I don't reckon they'll find any papers here, whatever Mistress Crichlow's said. And they've not asked after – after the lads.

MARGERY [*Pause*] He's gone already. Of course. Do you know where?

ROGER Tom took him, but he'll not stay there, I know that. Back down south, I should think.

MARGERY [*Makes towards stairs*] I need to turn out the chamber. Sir Philip's asking when we want him buried. He's been poking about and all. I didn't say, I thought Master Tom would settle that. Only I wondered about –

ROGER Don't fret. There's a priest in Lancaster as knows and he'll do the necessary when he can.

MARGERY [*Sits*] They've all gone. The master and Father Edward and – and Fulk. And Will. They've all gone. What do we do, then?

ROGER You knew he'd go back.

MARGERY Ay, I knew. Is that supposed to help me?

ROGER Come on, love. Like you said, they come and go. Don't get me wrong, but we've all had too much happening these last months, and now Master Alex is gone, God rest him, and old Hastings or whoever he really is – not that I'm glad he's in those bastards' hands in London, but you know what I mean...

MARGERY I don't think so. I don't think so. You might not have noticed but things don't go backwards. Will used to say that, when Father Edward tried to tell us it would be all right once the Queen or someone like that had seen the light. You... you see something as was covered up before, and you think, it doesn't have to be this, I don't have to be this, I can dig inwards and find what I never met before and you can't stop seeing it. Or I can look at you, Roger Livesey, and think, God, what's in there, then, if you start digging? [*Half-laughing*] What's going on behind that grey face, maybe it's all festivals and dances in there, only he never lets it out and perhaps he's laughing inside at the rest of us. And when I see him, I think, Christ, I don't know him, though I see him every day of my bloody life. And that makes everything, makes it, I don't know, more dangerous, more, more...

ROGER What the hell are you on about?

MARGERY Forget it, Rodge. Having you on, you silly old bugger. But still. What do we do, eh? When we know there's something behind the curtains. Behind the – eyes. Father Edward had an answer. You peel yourself down when you confess and then you dress up again only you dress up in what he tells you to wear and you turn into someone new who does all the right stuff and tells their beads and signs the pledges to pray and goes to Mass and keeps away from the parish church and has a list of saints to help you along for every day of the week. Always someone to tell you who you are in case you forget, shove your name in front of you with a list of your jobs. Only, like, like Will used to say: when you know you're choosing it, you know you don't *have* to choose it and it's another kind of play, another set of curtains and you're still nowhere nearer who you are.

ROGER So he wasn't much use sorting it out either, was he?

MARGERY Who said you could sort it? But you have to look at it. Inside, outside, you have to look at it. No-one to tell you who you are, but you can look. That's what he thought. [*Pause*] But you know something, Roger, you can drown that way, like you want to jump into a river if you look long enough from the bridge. Jump into the dark inside you and everyone else. Like he did with Margaret and me. And whatever else he did.

ROGER Don't blame him for all this; it was bloody Meg, you know that.

MARGERY Sometimes I imagine him talking to her, looking into the river of her, jumping in before he knew what he was doing. Betraying someone in his sleep. And is that when who you are comes through, then, when you're asleep? Sleepwalking? Oh God, I'm losing it. [*Stands, walks up and down a couple of times, hands against sides*] Sorry Rodge. You don't deserve all this.

ROGER Talk away, love. We're all at sea these days.

MARGERY At sea. Ay, that's it. You can remember what it was like to stand on solid ground, only there isn't any to be had any longer; and you look over the side when the wind drops and see your face and a great empty sky behind it. [*Silence*] I was going upstairs. Clean around a bit. Stop thinking who's not here, isn't that right?

ROGER [*With effort*] All right. Say you… you look over the side, like you say. And you don't just see your face but… other folk's faces. All at sea, eh? All of us, you, me, Will, Edward. And the ship… goes on, like. And what you can trust is the wood and the nails and the sailcloth.

MARGERY Christ, Roger! You can turn it when you've a mind to.

ROGER No, I don't rightly know what I'm saying, love. But does either of them need to be right, Edward or Will? Or Mistress bloody Crichlow? Or the Queen or the agents or the King of Spain or... The ship's going and one day it's going to run aground on the side of a little bank of earth six feet long, every bloody soul on board.

MARGERY Ay, well. But folk won't stop looking over the side. And they'll think like Father Edmund, what's down there, what keeps it all moving, or they'll think like Will, is that really my face in the water or his or hers next to me and how do you know the difference. [*Pause; then half-laugh*] So it doesn't get quiet on board.

ROGER Not drowned yet, eh? It's a start, love. Keep at it, so you don't get drawn to jump overboard; keep singing so the sea doesn't get into your lungs, is that it? Do you reckon they'll keep singing? Edward and Will? When Edward's under the butcher's cleaver? Or Will making gloves with his dad in the Midlands and saving money to pay for whatever poor cow he's got pregnant and wondering what he could have been if he'd stayed here or gone overseas with the Company or whatever?

MARGERY Singing doesn't come easy to anyone these days, far as I can tell. I reckon we need the nails and the cloth and what not. But it's worth listening out for. 'Cause when folk do sing in times like this, maybe it's worth stopping for.

ROGER Bloody times; that's what Alex would say.

MARGERY He wasn't wrong. Only when are they not? [*Pause*] I've got to clear the chamber.

[*She starts up the stairs, leaving Roger seated. From above, she starts singing, 'In youth, when I did love'; Roger smiles wryly, sits and listens to the first verse, then joins in the second verse as he walks off stage and Margery begins to come down the stairs, arms loaded with bed linen; the lights fade to blackout as she finishes the song, alone.*]

In youth when I did love, did love,
Methought it was very sweet,
To contract, O, the time for my behove,
Methought there was nothing more meet.

But age with his stealing steps
Hath clawed me in his clutch,
And hath shipped me intil the land,
As if I had never been such.

A pickaxe and a spade, a spade,
For and a shrouding sheet,
O and a pit of clay for to be made
For such a guest is meet.

Rowan Williams was the 104th Archbishop of Canterbury, and is acknowledged internationally as an outstanding theological writer and scholar. He has written extensively in philosophy, theology (especially early and patristic Christianity), spirituality and religious aesthetics. He is author of many books, including *On Christian Theology* (2000); *The Sound of Knowledge: Christian Spirituality from the New Testament to St John of the Cross* (2003); *Grace and Necessity: Reflections on Art and Love* (2006); and *The Edge of Words: God and the Habits of Language* (2014). He is currently Master of Magdalene College, Cambridge.

Epilogue
Some Further Account of the Life &c. of Mr. William Shakespear, with Corrections Made to the First and Second Editions, and with the Supplementation of New Matter Acquir'd from Diligent Researches in the Publick Records, and from Conversations Mr. Betterton had with the people of Stratford-upon-Avon (1715)

Edited by Graham Holderness[1]

IT seems to be a kind of Respect due to the Memory of Excellent Men, especially of those whom their Wit and Learning have made Famous, to deliver some Account of themselves, as well as their Works, to Posterity. For this Reason, how fond do we see some People of discovering any little Personal Story of the great Men of Antiquity, their Families, the common Accidents of their Lives, and even their Shape, Make and Features have been the Subject of critical Enquiries. How trifling soever this Curiosity may seem to be, it is certainly very Natural; and we are hardly satisfy'd with an Account of any remarkable Person, 'till we have heard him describ'd even to the very Cloaths he wears. As for what relates to Men of Letters, the knowledge of an Author may sometimes conduce to the better understanding his Book.

Notes for this section can be found on page 129.

He was the Son of Mr. *John Shakespear*, and was Born at *Stratford* upon *Avon*, in *Warwickshire*, in *April* 1564. His Family were of good Figure and Fashion there, and are mention'd as Gentlemen. By his own father's Estate, *John Shakespear* was a husbandman, but the son being possess'd of that Resourcefulness that can make a Marchaunt of a Farmer, grew to be a substantial Dealer and Tradesman of the town. Husbandry being his orginall Calling, John dealt in the Carkasses of beasts, and was by the Record of one who knew the Town and its inhabitants well, a Butcher. Finding that the Cloathing of sheep and cattle afforded more Profitable and respectable Employment than the butchering of their Edible parts, he became a *whyttawer*, a species of Tanner, engaged in the Whitening and Softening of Leather, the better to adapt its substance to the Manufacture of Shoes, Belts, Purses, Satchels, Sword-hangers and Gloves, and a considerable Dealer in Wool. In this noisome and noxious Trade, the poet's Father found his Craft and refined his Art, for from the Leather cured and prepar'd in his Workshop, he fell to fashioning Fine Gloves, and soon began to prosper at the Trade. It is without Controversie that Mr. *Shakespear* is recorded and remembered as a Glover of *Stratford*. His name is subscribed as Glover in the Register and Publick Writings relating to that Town, and Archdeacon *Plume* of *Rochester* had it of *Sir John Mennis*[2] that he well remembered *Mr. Shakespear* in his glover's shop, a merry-cheeked old Man who spoke well tho' boldly of his Celebrated son. My Will, he said, is an Honest fellow, with a place at Court, but never too Lofty to crack a Jest with his old Dad.

John Shakespear's dwelling-place in *Stratford* was long known as the Woolshop, tho' 'tis now partly an Inn, and partly a Butcher's shop in which is continued *John Shakespear's* native trade. This same inn lies under the Sign of the Swan and Maidenhead, which Emblem remembers both our Illustrious poet, and his more Glorious patroness the Queene, of whom more Herafter. A gentleman of my Acquaintance had it from the Landlord that beneath the Boards of the parlour Floor, when rais'd, were found the Remnants of Wool, and the Refuse of Wool-combing embedded with the Earth. I am told of a record in the Court of Common Pleas that has Mr. *Shakespear* suing one *John Walford*, a clothier, for negligence in payment of £21 for 21 tods of Wool, tho' I know not if't be true. True it is that in another Court *John Shakespear* brought Action against *Henry Field* a tanner for the price of some Barley. The Difference they must have

Mended, for *Shakespear* was an Executor to *Field's* will.³ This *Field* was father to *Richard*, who was Prentic'd to a London stationer, and afterwards a Printer, and who succeeded on his Master's death to both his Wife, a comely French woman, and his Business. 'Twas from Richard's press came our poet's *Venus and Adonis*, in which Poem there is also some little Difference of Years between the Lady and her young Man. These two School-fellows of Stratford worked each in his father's Trade, and many are of the opinion that the sons of Tanners and Butchers have so little access to Learning, that 'tis a wonder any one of them should do Well. Yet *Field* was preferr'd to a London Printer, and *Shakespear* was advanced to the foremost Theatre of the City. It is my Conjecture that both their Fathers were wont to Supply, of their Workshops, to the London Stationers and Printers, fine Parchments and Vellums made from the skins of their Sheep, Goats and Calves. And this, tho' I own 'tis but my Belief, is how these country boys wrote their Names in History, by first writing them on Parchments made in their fathers' Shops. 'Is not parchment', asks Hamlet, 'made of sheep-skins?' Horatio replies, 'Ay, my Lord. And calf-skins too'. That Speech of High style made by *Shakespear* in the killing of a Calf, he may have committed to Writing on vellum made from the same Creature's skin. Certain it is that his Plays abound with knowledge of these Crafts: of Hides, of Calf-skins, Sheep-skins, Lamb-skins, Fox-skins; of Dog-skins, Deer-skins and Cheveril; of Neat's-leather shoes, and Sheeps'-leather bridles; of Horse-hair and Calves' guts, Aprons, Bottles and Jerkins of leather, Greasy fells and White fleeces.

Though a substantial Marchaunt and Burgess of the town, John *Shakespear* had so large a Family, not ten (as I wrote in my first edition, as I had the number from Mr. *Betterton*, who has since read the record with a closer scrutiny), but eight, that tho' *William* was his eldest Son, he could give him no better Education than his own Employment. He had bred him, 'tis true, for some time at a Free-School, where 'tis probable he acquir'd that little *Latin* he was Master of: But the narrowness of his Circumstances, and the want of his assistance at Home, forc'd his Father to withdraw him from thence, and unhappily prevented his further Proficiency in that Language. It is certain that the Neighbours of Stratford heretofore told unto Mr. *Aubrey* that *Shakespear*, as a boy, Practising his father's trade of Butchery, when he killed a Calf, would do it in a *high style*, and make a Speech. Whence he had these Speeches, I know not, for it is without

Controversie that he had no knowledge of the Writings of the Antient Poets, as in his Works themselves we find no traces of any thing that looks like an Imitation of 'em. Some *Latin* without question he did know, and may have Employed some snatches of Cicero or Caesar, remembered out of his Grammar, in his Calf-killing. Or some fine words out of his Bible may have served as Fitting accompaniment to the Slaughtering, as the words used by Abraham and Aaron, when they served so a Ram, or a fatted Calf. Certain it is that no Regularity and Deference for the ancients restrain'd that Fire, Impetuosity, and even beautiful Extravagance which we admire in *Shakespear*, and which in my Opinion furnished him with ample Eloquence with which to Beautify the Slaughterhouse, and to make a Theatre of a Shambles. See how Piteously he recalls, in his *Second Part of Henry the Sixt*, the Cruelty of the Abbatoir:

> And as the butcher takes away the calf,
> And binds the wretch, and beats it when it strays, ...
> And as the dam runs lowing up and down,
> Looking the way her harmless young ones went,
> And can do naught but wail her darling's loss ...

Upon his leaving School, he seems to have given intirely into that way of Living which his Father propos'd to him; and in order to settle in the World after a Family manner, he thought fit to marry while he was yet very Young. His Wife was the Daughter of one *Hathaway*, said to have been a substantial Yeoman in the Neighbourhood of *Stratford*. In this kind of Settlement he continu'd for some time, 'till an Extravagance that he was guilty of, forc'd him both out of his Country and that way of Living which he had taken up. He made a frequent practice of Deer-stealing, robbing a Park that belong'd to *Sir Thomas Lucy of Cherlecot*, near *Stratford*. There be some have Question'd this story, as the account of a Misdemeanour alien to the Character of our gentle Poet. But at that time *Sir Thomas* had no Royal licence to keep a park at *Charlecote*, for 'twas some years after this that his fields were Empaled. The free-warren of his land sheltered many Beasts of the chase, as Rabbits and Hares, Pheasants and Deer, and of these the good people of *Stratford* had for many years made their choice, remembering the Rights of the Free-born Englishman, and taking such prey as suited them from under the Keeper's winking eye. It is certain that the young *Shakespear* took his Share, for a jolly old Parson of *Oxford* noted down that he was much given to Stealing Venison and Rabbits from *Sir Thomas Lucy's* lands.

The Flesh of these beasts gave sustenance to his growing flock of Children, and the Pelts furnish'd his father's workshop with skin enough for many a fine pair of Gloves.

Sir Thomas liked this despoiling of his Land by the people so little that he resolv'd to make Example of one, and had his Keepers lie in wait for *Shakespear*, one night when Moonlight whitened the Turf. Our Poet, wandering idly in the Greenwood, and Wounding the barks of trees with his Love-sonnets, was easily Caught, and afterwards Whipped and held for a time in the County gaol. Angered beyond Measure by the Knight's tyrannical Usage, *Shakespear* composed a Bitter Ballad, mocking Sir Thomas as a Covetous Cuckold, who needed not to keep Horns in his Park, since his wife bestowed them so liberally on his Head. This Ballad was writ upon a sheet of Parchment made by *Shakespear* himself from the skin of a stolen Sheep, and stuck upon *Sir Thomas's* Park gate. At this *Sir Thomas* was Angry out of all Compass, and would have prosecuted *Shakespear* even more Severely, and so he was Oblig'd to leave his Business and Family in Warwickshire, for some time, and shelter himself in London. In due time he took further Revenges, for in *The Merry Wives of Windsor*, he has made Falstaff a Deer-stealer, that he might at the same time remember his *Warwickshire* Prosecutor, under the Name of Justice *Shallow*; he has given him very near the same Coat of Arms which *Dugdale*, in his Antiquities of that County describes for a Family there.[4]

It is at this Time, and upon this Accident, that he is said to have made his first Acquaintance in the Play-house. He was receiv'd into the Company then in being, at first in a very mean Rank, as a Serviture, for what was he at this time, for all his Promise, but a Butcher's Prentice run away from his master? When he came to London, he was without Money and Friends, being a Stranger he knew not by what means to support Himself. At that time as Gentlemen were accustomed to ride to the Playhouse, *Shakespear*, driven to the last Necessity, went to the Playhouse door, and pick'd up a little Money by holding the Horses of those who had no Servants, that they might be ready again after the Performance. If this sounds too Menial an occupation for our greatest Man of Letters, then heed the witness of another, who records that *Shakespear* took good Care of the Gentlemen's Horses who came to the Play. Who better to bestow such Care on Animals, than one whose family Depended on 'em, and who from his apprenticeship knew well how to Soothe a fearful Nag, or quiet a restless Jade? Though some speak scornfully of this Tale, and cannot bide the thought of their *Shakespear* splashing in those Manured Precincts, it was no mean Craft that he assumed, there at the Theatre door, and soon became Eminent in that Profession. But his admirable Wit, and the natural Turn of it to the Stage, soon distinguished him, if not as an extraordinary Actor, yet as an excellent Writer. For he knew as well, remarked one clever Fellow, the inside of a beast as he knew the Outside, and could draw you out a sheet of Vellum as handily as he could hold your Horse for the length of a Play. And did not *Shakespear* himself speak of 'a wit of cheveril, that stretches from an inch narrow to an ell broad', as if to him the Stretching of Imagination, and the Pulling into shape of fine Leather, were actions Comparable, and not utterly Distinct? Being come of a simple and industrious Kind, neither arrogant nor froward in their Manners, besides the advantages of his Wit, he was in himself a good-natur'd Man, of great sweetness, and a most agreeable Companion; so that it is no wonder if with so many good Qualities he made himself acquainted with the best Conversations of those Times. Queen *Elizabeth* had several of his Plays Acted before her, and without doubt gave him many gracious Marks of her Favour. She used frequently to appear upon the Stage before the audience, or to sit delighted behind the Scenes. Once when *Shakespear* was personating the part of a King, she crossed the Stage when he was Performing, but he did not Notice it! Accordingly, as he was about to make his Exit, she Stepped before him, dropped her Glove, and re-crossed the Stage, which *Shakespear* noticing, immediately presented the Glove to the Queen. Her Majesty, being perhaps a little Displeas'd that the actor had paid more Attention to his audience than to his Sovereign, or rather loving (as she did) a cruel Jest even more than she loved her Poet-favourite, was heard to say: 'Gramercy, good Master *Shakespear*, of the glove. Tell me, *is it one that you made yourself?*' Which shaft of Wit, glancing thus upon his Humble origins, so deeply distressed him that he left the Stage, and never again return'd.[5]

The latter Part of his Life was spent at his native *Stratford*, as all Men of good Sense will wish theirs may be, in Ease, Retirement, and the Conversation of his Friends, the Shopkeepers and Merchants, the Tradesmen and Craftsmen, the Butcher, the Baker, &c. He had the good Fortune to gather an Estate equal to his Occasion, and, in that, to his Wish. His pleasurable Wit, and good Nature, engag'd him in the Acquaintance, and entitled him to the Friendship of the Gentlemen of the Neighbourhood.

He Dy'd in the 53d Year of his Age, and was bury'd on the North side of the Chancel, in the Great Church at Stratford, where a Monument is plac'd in the Wall. How apt a Likeness this is, I know not, though many Condemn it as unworthy its great Subject. One Gentleman, visiting the Church, was heard to say, intending to the Disparagement of the Sculptor, that to his eye it looked not so much like a Poet, as like a self-satisfied Pork Butcher. But how indeed should our *Shakespear* look, this Butcher's boy become the world's greatest Poet, if not, at least a little, like a Butcher? and if not, at least a little, satisfied with himself?

Graham Holderness is the author or editor of some 60 books of literary criticism, theory, scholarship and theology; 'creative criticism'; and creative writing in fiction, poetry and drama. Key critical works include *The Shakespeare Myth* (MUP, 1988) *The Politics of Theatre and Drama* (Routledge, 1992); *Shakespeare: The Histories* (Bloomsbury, 2000) and *The Faith of William Shakespeare* (Lion Books, 2016). Works of creative criticism, which are half criticism and half fiction, include *Nine Lives of William Shakespeare* (Bloomsbury/Arden Shakespeare, 2011); *Tales from Shakespeare: Creative Collisions* (Cambridge, 2014) and *Re-writing Jesus: Christ in 20th Century Fiction and Film* (Bloomsbury, 2014). He has published a poetry collection *Craeft: Poems from the Anglo-Saxon* (Beeston: Shoestring Press, 2001), and four works of fiction: *The Prince of Denmark* (University of Hertfordshire Press, 2001); *Ecce Homo* (Bloomsbury, 2014); *Black and Deep Desires: William Shakespeare Vampire Hunter* (Top Hat Books, 2015); and *Meat, Murder, Malfeasance, Medicine and Martyrdom: Smithfield Stories* (Brighton: EER, 2019).

Notes

1. In my opinion this document is a manifest forgery, since it contains material of which Rowe in his first edition shows no knowledge, and incorporates anecdotes not available at the time of its supposed publication . – Ed.
2. Sir John had a remarkable memory, as he was two years old when John Shakespeare died. –Ed.
3. Not quite: he helped to appraise Field's goods after his death. – Ed.

4. Sir William Dugdale, *Antiquities of Warwickshire. Illustrated from Records, Leiger-Books, Manuscripts, Charters, Evidences, Tombes, and Armes. Beautified with maps, prospects, and portraictures* (1656).
5. The incorporation of this tradition gives a terminus a quo for the forgery, which cannot have been undertaken any earlier than 1825. The story was published in Richard Ryan's *Dramatic Table Talk; or Scenes, Situations & Adventures, Serious & Comic, in Theatrical History & Biography* (London: John Knight & Henry Lacy, 1825) vol 2, pp. 156–7. Ryan's version of the anecdote ends quite differently, with the Queen 'greatly pleased with his [Shakespeare's] behaviour'. – Ed.

Index

A

Anamorphosis, 47-51, 57
Arnold, Matthew, 59-61
Athenaeum Club, 59
Aubrey, John, 78, 125
Austen, Jane, 59, 61

B

Baddesley, Clinton, 40, 55
Baker, Mary, 27-28, 39, 52, 128
Barton, Anne, 3, 6
Bate, Jonathan, 79
Beetz, K.H., 62
Blind, Mathilde, 65-66
Boyd, William, 3
Braddocks, 43, 55
Bradford, Richard, 69
Branagh, Kenneth, 66
Braudel, Fernand, 60
British Library, iv, 65
Brophy, John, 31, 37
Browning, Robert, 22, 59, 61
Burbage, Richard, 8, 18, 68
Burgess, Anthony, 7, 14-18, 23, 31, 36-37, 125
Bushwood Hall, 40

C

Campaspe (John Lyly), 69
Campion, Edmund, 5, 42, 53, 55-56, 64, 79-80, 110
Chambers, E.K., 39, 60, 76
Charlecote, Warwickshire, 6, 76, 126
Churchill, Winston, 64
Coriolanus, 67, 73, 75
Cottam, John, 79, 81-83, 86-89, 94, 98, 109, 117
Cottam, Thomas, 79
Coughton Court, 43-45, 55-56
Cromwell, Oliver, 64
Crumme, Hannah Leah, 65

D

Domesticity, 4, 25-26, 28-29, 31-33
Duffy, Carol Ann, 32, 37
Dugdale, Sir William, 127, 130
Duncan-Jones, Katherine, 8, 20-21, 24, 79

E

Edel, Leon, 59
Eliot, T.S., 7, 10-11, 22, 59, 62
Elizabeth I, 45, 52, 73, 79
Ellman, Richard, 59-60
Elton, Ben, 65-66
Elton, Geoffrey, 66
Everett, Barbara, 6, 19

F

Fairfax-Lucy, Alice, 6
Fielitz, Sonja, v, 4, 38, 40, 42, 44, 46, 48, 50-52, 54, 56
Fisher, Edward, 31, 37
Folger Shakespeare Library, 64
Freed, Amy, 32
Fripp, Edgar Innes, 60

G

Garnet, Henry, 42, 46, 55
Gastrell, Francis, 35
Gillom, Fulke, 78, 80, 86
Greenblatt, Stephen, 20, 24, 39, 53, 64, 66, 69
Greene, Robert, 9, 21, 50, 66
Greer, Germaine, 25, 35, 37
Gunpowder Plot, 40, 43-45, 55

H

Halliwell-Phillips, James
Harris, Frank, 69
Harvington Hall, 48, 51, 56
Hathaway, Anne, v, 4, 6, 14, 25-37
Hathaway, Anne, Cottage, 28
Hawkes, Terry, 70
Hesketh, Sir Thomas, 78, 117
Hindlip House, 45
Hocke, Gustav Réné, 49, 57
Hoghton Tower, 78-80
Hoghton, Alexander, 78-81
Holbein, Hans the Younger, 78-80
Holderness, Graham, 3, 5, 29, 36-37, 39, 123-129
Holland, Peter, vi, 4, 63-64, 66-67
Honan, Park, v, vii, 4, 20, 24, 58-62, 69

I

Ignatius of Loyola, 71
Illusion, 12, 46-48, 50-51, 56
Irvine, William, 61

J

Jauss, Hans Robert, 8, 20-21, 24
Jesuits, 38, 41, 43, 46, 51, 53-56, 79
Johnson, Samuel, 70
Joyce, James, 36, 59-60

K

Kelly, Tim, 30, 37

L

Lanier, Douglas, 19, 24, 29, 37
Laughton, Charles, 63
London, 2, 6, 8, 14, 16-17, 21-24, 29-30, 33-34, 36-37, 40, 42, 52-56, 58-59, 61, 65, 72-73, 75-77, 93-94, 100, 116, 119, 125, 127, 129-130
Lord Strange, Earl of Derby, 78
Lucy, Sir Thomas, 126
Lyly, John, 68

M

Madden, John (*Shakespeare in Love*), 18-19
Malone, Edmond, 2, 60
Maltby, Arthur, 61
Manningham, John, 68
Marchand, Leslie A., 59
Marlowe, Christopher, v, 4, 7-24, 53, 56, 60-61, 65, 71-72
Matisse, Henri, 58
Matthew, Colin, 64
Mitchell, David, 65-67
Murdoch, Iris, 68

N

New Criticism, 59
Nicoll, Charles, 29, 37
Norman, Marc, 3, 18, 24
Nye, Robert, 3, 32, 36-37

O

O'Toole, Peter, 63
Ovid, Metamorphoses, 42, 51
Owen, Nicholas, v, 38, 41-46, 48, 50-51, 55, 57

P

Peterson, Audrey, 30, 37
Potter, Lois, vi, 4-5, 68, 70-71
priest holes, 41-43, 45, 48, 50-51, 55-57

R

Ray, Gordon N., 78, 80, 86
Red Lion Theatre, 61
Ribner, Irving, 7, 11-14, 22
Robeson, Paul, 63
Rooke, Leon, 6
Rowe, Nicholas, 1, 3, 5-6, 63, 76, 129
Ryan, Richard, 130

D

Sawyer, Robert, 4, 7-24
Scheil, Katherine, 4, 25-37, 39
Schoenbaum, Samuel, 4, 22, 59-60, 63-65, 67, 75-76
Shakeshafte, William, vi, 5, 39, 53, 78-81, 83, 85-87, 89, 91, 93, 95, 97, 99, 101, 103, 105, 107, 109, 111, 113, 115, 117, 119, 121
Shakespeare Birthplace Trust, 26-28, 35, 65
Shakespeare, John, 31, 40, 54, 129
Shakespeare, Judith, 33, 37
Shakespeare, William
- and religion, v, 4, 14, 16, 18, 38-39, 41, 43, 45, 47, 49, 51-55, 57, 79, 85, 87, 93, 98, 100, 105, 111-112, 114
- and will
    - individual plays:
        — *Antony and Cleopatra*, 50
        — *Macbeth*, 8, 13, 46, 53, 73, 75
        — *Hamlet*, 11, 46, 53, 58, 64, 70, 73, 75, 125
    — *Henry the Sixth, Part 2*, 28, 126
    — *A Midsummer Night's Dream*, 67
    — *Othello*, 54, 63, 71, 73
        — *Richard II*, 8, 49-50, 54
        — *Romeo and Juliet*, 3, 13, 73, 75, 77
    — *The Taming of the Shrew*, 29, 75
    — *The Tempest*, 59, 73
    — *Titus Andronicus*, 15, 28
        — *Troilus and Cressida*, 50
        — *Twelfth Night*, 50, 69, 71, 73, 75
    — *Two Gentlemen of Verona*, 59
        — *The Winter's Tale*, 50, 57

Shapiro, James, 1, 6, 20, 24, 64
Southwell, Robert, 42, 44, 52, 55
Stonor, 56
Stoppard, Tom, 3, 18, 24
Strachey, Lytton, 63
Stratford-upon-Avon, vi, 4, 6, 40-41, 44, 63, 66-67, 72-75
Swinburne, Algernon Charles, 7, 9-10, 21-22

T

The Return from Parnassus, 68
Thiessen, Vern, 3
Throckmorton family, 44-45
Tiffany, Grace, 3, 32, 37
Trompe l'oeil, 47-49, 51, 56-57

U

University College London, 77

V

Virgil, 42, 68
Virgil, *Aeneid*, 42

W

Washington DC, 54, 60
Watson, Nicola J., 29, 36-37
Weis, Rene, 4-5, 72-77
Whelan, Peter, 3
Wilder, Thornton, 79
Williams, Rowan, vi, 5, 78, 80, 82, 84, 86, 88, 90, 92, 94, 96, 98, 100, 102, 104, 106, 108, 110, 112, 114, 116, 118, 120, 122
Winslett, Kate, 68

www.ingramcontent.com/pod-product-compliance
Lightning Source LLC
Chambersburg PA
CBHW070045120526
44589CB00035B/2325